WATERTRAIL

WATERTRAIL

THE

HIDDEN

PATH

THROUGH

PUGET

SOUND

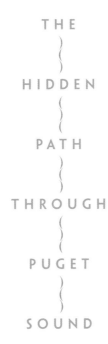

JOEL W. ROGERS

SASQUATCH BOOKS

SEATTLE

Printed in Hong Kong.
Distributed in Canada by Raincoast Books Ltd.
02 01 00 99 98   5 4 3 2 1

Book design by Karen Schober
Interior map illustration by Jonathan Combs

Front cover: John Larson and Scott Wellsandt off D'Arcy Island at sunrise,
with San Juan Island and Mount Baker in the distance.

Library of Congress Cataloging in Publication Data
Rogers, Joel W., 1947-
          Watertrail: the hidden path through Puget Sound/Joel Rogers.
               p.   cm.
Includes bibliographical references.
ISBN 1-57061-095-9
1. Puget Sound (Wash.)—Description of travel. 2. Canoes and canoeing—
Washington (State)—Puget Sound. 3. Cascadia Marine Trail (Wash.) 4. Rogers, Joel
W., 1947– —Journeys—Washington (State)—Puget Sound. I. Title
F879.P9R65 1998
917.97'7—dc21   97-46783

Sasquatch Books
615 Second Avenue
Seattle, Washington 98104
(206) 467-4300
books@sasquatchbooks.com
http://www.sasquatchbooks.com

*Sasquatch Books publishes high-quality adult nonfiction and children's books related to
the Northwest (Alaska to San Francisco). For more information about our titles, contact
us at the address above, or view our site on the World Wide Web.*

ACKNOWLEDGMENTS

The experience of researching this book was marked by an unhesitating interest from everyone I contacted. Agencies responded instantly, researchers dug for old theses, and individuals readily related their stories. Each referred me to others in the ever-expanding community of scientists, historians, fishers, mariners, paddlers, and friends dedicated to the preservation of Puget Sound and our marine habitat. Thank you for your work, your resolution, and your help.

Point Roberts •   *Boundary Bay*

GULF
ISLANDS

Georgia Strait

Saturna
Island   Patos
                Island   • *Alden Bank*

VANCOUVER
ISLAND

Boundary Pass

Waldron
Island   • **Bellingham**

Stuart   Orcas
Island   Island   Island   Lummi

SAN JUAN ISLANDS

Jones Island

Roche Harbor •   Cypress
                        Shaw   Island
D'Arcy   Island   Guemes
Island   San Juan   Island   • Saddlebag Island
            Island   • Friday   *Padilla*
                          Harbor   **Anacortes** • *Bay*   *Skagit River*

            Lime •   Lopez
            Kiln Point   Island   *Swinomish Channel*

Victoria •   *Cattle Pass*   Deception
                                                           Pass   • **La Conner**

                                                Rosario Strait   *Skagit Estuary*

Strait of Juan de Fuca   Whidbey
                                                  Island

                                      Fort Ebey •   Camano
                                                           Saratoga Passage   Island

Dungeness Spit

Port Angeles •   Point Wilson •
                                                  Port Townsend •

                                                  Marrowstone
                                                  Island   • **Everett**

                                                           Admiralty Inlet

OLYMPIC PENINSULA
                                                           • Point No Point

                                                  Kingston •

                                                           Puget Sound

                                                                      Ballard

                                      Hood Canal   Bainbridge
                                                          Island   *Elliott*
                                                                          Bay   • **Seattle**

                                      Bremerton •

                                                  Blake
                                                  Island

                                                           Puget Sound

PACIFIC OCEAN

                                                  Vashon
                                                  Island
                                      Burton

                                                  Maury
                                                  Island

CANADA

WASHINGTON

OREGON

                                      Pickering   *Case Inlet*   Kopachuck
                                      Passage   *Wollochet*
                                                  Key Peninsula   *Carr Inlet* *Bay*   • **Tacoma**

                                      Hartstene
                                      Island   *The Narrows*

                                                           McNeil
                                      Squaxin   Island
                                      Island
                                                  Anderson
                                                  Island

Budd Inlet

• **Olympia**

CONTENTS

In the fall of 1989, twenty-five people gathered at the Mountaineers Club in Seattle to discuss establishing a water trail through Puget Sound. Kayakers, canoeists, Washington Kayak Club members and Mountaineers members, they were drawn together by longtime kayaker Tom Deschner to meet a representative from the Washington State Department of Natural Resources (DNR), Michael Gruber. A recent transplant from the Eastern seaboard, Gruber described how a group of boaters in Maine, faced with too many people and too little public recreation land, had pioneered the 325-mile-long Maine Island Trail. The vision of a similar water trail here galvanized the group, and thus began the creation of the Cascadia Marine Trail.

The meeting participants formed an organization called the Washington Water Trails Association (WWTA). Over the next three years, the WWTA mapped out possible sites, garnered funds from corporate supporters including Recreational Equipment Incorporated (REI) and Starbucks Coffee, tinkered with waterless toilets, and learned how to lobby. Tom Steinburn, Sandie Nelson-Rumble, and other WWTA members made endless trips to the state capital to meet with representatives from the State Parks and Recreation Commission and the Department of Natural Resources, convincing them to accommodate those who chose human-powered watercraft to explore the state's marine parks system. In January 1993 the agencies and WWTA came to an agreement, and the initial twenty sites were designated.

Today, with the cooperation of the State Parks Commission, the DNR, county and city governments, and private property owners, WWTA members and staff maintain and continue to expand the Cascadia Marine Trail. Ultimately, it is these organizations and volunteers who provide a growing freedom for paddlers on the waters of Puget Sound and beyond. It is to the creators of the Cascadia Marine Trail that *Watertrail: The Hidden Path Through Puget Sound* is dedicated.

—*Joel W. Rogers, Seattle, 1998*

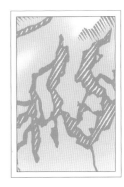

The scenic details of Budd Inlet revealed themselves in all their early-morning glory: ragged lines of pilings from long-ago mills, the rotting keels of beached boats, and the Capitol dome rising over the town of Olympia. The inlet, lined with wharves and piers, lay perfectly still—disturbed only by the stately movement of Canada geese. The flock, gliding across the water like a flotilla of warships on the incoming tide, broke the

A TIDE OF ORIGINS

silence with low snorts and calls. They hesitated and shied away on seeing me, my kayak, and the brightly colored dry bags I had strewn on the barnacled rocks.

With an urgency familiar from years of racing the tide, I loaded my kayak one dry bag ahead of the flood. With each carry from solid ground to intertidal zone, I sank deeper into a fine and ancient mixture of glacial silt, cellulose, and crustacea. Shifting my weight from one slowly sinking foot to the other, I packed bow and stern, my kayak accepting the gear, safety equipment, ten days of food, and a smattering of mud with equanimity.

My kayak is officially named *Eugene Odum,* after the Georgia biologist who did pioneering research on estuaries and environmental science. But over time and trips, and for the sake of brevity and affection, the *Eugene Odum* has come to be known as "Boato." With a deck the color of a glacier-green sea and a hull of battleship gray, Boato is no

A half cup of coffee and a full
Boato meet the Budd Inlet tide.

stranger to nasty put-ins. She and I have launched from the ice-choked beaches of Alaska's Glacier Bay and from the slippery kelp-covered rocks of Canada's Queen Charlotte Islands. For sixteen years we have been trashed in the dumping waves of Washington's wilderness waters as well as the coastal waters of Oregon, California, and sunny Baja. Yet Boato and I have largely ignored Puget Sound, our "home" water, considering it more of a ferry ride to other adventures, a body of water to travel around rather than a destination to be paddled, weathered, understood.

Boato now nearly afloat, I shoved her into the Sound, feeling a pure and rare joy as I launched this solo trip. I had a solid month to kayak the Sound, to veer into its smallest bays and backwaters, to make open-water crossings through areas busy with shipping, to camp nightly along its shore, and to watch vessel traffic and the transit of wildlife with full, unhurried freedom.

For decades it had been impossible to do this, to negotiate the length of Puget Sound in a human-powered craft. Great stretches of the coast had become a NO TRESPASSING shoreline of private homes and property that proved a barrier to paddlers requiring a safe campsite. But the new sport of sea kayaking inspired both the idea and the volunteers to build a trail of secure sites through Puget Sound and the San Juan Islands. In January 1993, with the cooperation of state and local governments, the volunteers now known as the Washington Water Trails Association created the Cascadia Marine Trail System. Now kayakers, rowers, canoeists, and day sailors could travel a water trail stretching from the South Sound through Admiralty Inlet, into the San Juans, and on to the Canadian border. And I was to be one of the first to paddle the entire length of it, immersing myself in the blend of saltwater wilderness, history, and community that is the greater Puget Sound.

But as I contemplated the patchwork of mud, geese, and sun at Budd Inlet, I was mindful of the questions packed in with my sleeping bag and chart case: Would I still like

A PIONEER'S ARRIVAL

"It was a dreary, dark December day. It had rained considerably. The road from Tumwater to Olympia was ankle deep in mud and threaded a dense forest with a narrow track. With expectations raised at the idea of seeing the Capitol and chief town of the Territory, the weary travelers toiled up a small hill in the edge of the timber, reached the summit and eagerly looked to see the new metropolis. Their hearts sank with bitter disappointment as they surveyed the dismal and forlorn scene before them. A low, flat neck of land, running into the bay, down it stretched the narrow muddy track winding among the stumps, which stood thickly on either side. Twenty small houses bordered the road, while back of them on the left and next the shore were a number of Indian lodges, with canoes drawn up on the beach, and Indians and dogs lounging about."

Mrs. Isaac Ingalls Stevens, Olympia,
the Washington Territory, 1850

today's Puget Sound? Would there be enough wildness left in its sloughs, enough character in the wharves and waterways, enough of an awareness of the Sound itself amid the rising tide of waterfront homes and port cities? This was not just my preference for wilderness kayaking asserting itself, but a more visceral sensation. As a child growing up on its shores, I perceived the Sound as a seemingly indelible gift, a passage to adventure, proof of the wonder and durability of nature—my whole world. Now it had become a small, still beautiful but long-neglected, part of my life.

Would the experience of kayaking over four hundred miles, while remaining never more than a landing away from a grocery freezer filled with Ben & Jerry's Frozen Yogurt, be equal to the Sound of my youth? Sitting astride the cockpit, poling off the beach, I dragged my boots in the waters of Budd Inlet to wash off the mud, then slipped them beneath the deck and paddled off to find out.

Boris Trofimenko is a 280-foot factory trawler, Norwegian-designed, Spanish-built, managed by Americans and flagged and crewed by Russians. She fished off Kamchatka, her catch of pollock and cod bound for the Far East market. Ahead of her at a Port of Olympia pier was the log ship *Rubin Bonanza*, her bow facing the Capitol, her hull hemmed in by log rafts of old-growth fir bound for Japan. She too was foreign-flagged: Panama, with Japanese owners and a Philippine crew that must have been preparing for breakfast and the return of the longshore gangs as I approached. A small tug named *Cedar King,* with two men aboard, was on a converging course with me. She was pulling a log raft across the inlet, moving slowly, almost imperceptibly, with the immense weight of the timber in tow. I paddled out ahead and crossed the tug's bow, acknowledging the skipper with a wave as the *Cedar King*

A merchant ship's bow from a kayaker's perspective.

Deckhouse detail of a retired Red Stack tugboat.

churned by. It was as if I had paddled into a classic Elton Bennett silkscreen of the Northwest: gulls and tugboats, ships and cargo.

Olympia's first day as a port city began when the brig *Orbit* arrived on New Year's Day, 1850. The *Orbit* was the first commercial ship in Budd Inlet to load timber, and that January she sailed with logs for the piers of San Francisco and the orgy of construction that accompanied the frenzied California gold rush. On her return voyage she brought clothing, sugar, and miscellaneous supplies for the first pioneers in the Puget Sound region. She must have anchored somewhere near my course.

With a gentle stroke to starboard, I turned away from the ships and the ramshackle retail stores of the Olympia waterfront and steered beneath the outermost piers of the harbor, derelict for some years, the unsafe structure now a curious man-made nesting site for pigeon guillemots. Along the eastern shore I began to enjoy a well-treed, nearly house-free shoreline. Skimming over eelgrass, moving in and out of the sun at about the speed of a moderate walk, Boato and I took in new territory.

Budd Inlet is one of six inlets that carve the shores of southernmost Puget Sound. They are as narrow as the low, forested peninsulas separating them, north–south trending, gouged and elongated by the Pleistocene glaciers.

Here is the quiet part of the Sound, where the wind has to work its way between overhanging alders to touch the water, where the fine sand and clay banks are easily carved with initials and declarations of undying love, and just as easily weathered away. As I paddled down the inlet, I passed coves with 1920s- and 1930s-era summer houses in a tight jumble, followed by high-bank beach. In quick succession I saw deer silhouetted on the next point, a harbor seal surfacing off my left shoulder, a belted kingfisher flying ahead of me with a rattling call, and crows strutting about the beach ignoring my passage.

Three miles into the day's paddle there was a sudden break in the bluffs, revealing a heretofore-hidden bay named Gull Harbor with two stream-fed arms worth investigating. Pointing Boato in past a perfect set of small spits, I drifted, letting my momentum carry me deeper into the silence of a relatively untouched harbor. The beach had been logged in the 1800s, but the timber had now returned, hiding the few houses. Mature alder branched out over the beach, and a couple of well-used boats were secured to boom logs. I ruddered my kayak into the south arm, where it narrowed beneath enfolding spring-green trees. There, on the only open shore, stood a raccoon. Releasing my spray skirt while still drifting, I opened the dry bag between my legs and removed my camera, all the while watching this most omnivorous of vertebrates hunting, sampling, and eating whatever the beach provided. And all the while the raccoon monitored me, this long, low, floating object with a noisy center. I raised my camera, focused, corrected the meter, refocused, and shot. Hearing the sound of the shutter, my subject stared with a quiet dignity as I repacked my gear and backpaddled away.

| Procyon lotor *in Gull Harbor.*

I departed Gull Harbor feeling that despite my intrusion, my nosing about in the kelp, I had been accepted into the daily pattern of the South Sound's tides of life. The raccoon and the man in the kayak were a convocation of beachcombers, lending an enchanted air to the beginning of my trip.

Small, fleet, and quiet, the sea kayak, also called a touring kayak (and a "sea canoe" in Europe), is a hunting tool. It is a highly evolved example of the Arctic people's ingenuity: the Alaskan Aleut, Koniag, and Chugach of the Gulf of Alaska, the Kamchatka and Chutosk of the Siberian coast, and the Greenland

Fresh petroglyphs now grace Budd Inlet's silt and clay bluffs, the outwash of glaciers that retreated 14,000 years ago.

Thule Eskimo all developed skin boats. Once made of bone and driftwood, sea mammal sinew and hide, the exquisite designs have survived to be reborn in a new craft of fiberglass or wood, fabric, and aluminum or plastic.

Boato is a great and early example of the contemporary Northwest sea kayak designs. (Newer kayak designs adhere to a sleeker, faster, minimum-volume concept, much like the hunting boats of the Arctic.) Called a Polaris II, my kayak was designed in 1981 and built by Seattle's Dan Ruuska. Boato is a full-size 17-foot by 25½-inch, 42-pound hand-lay-up fiberglass single with simple yet elegant lines, fair sea-keeping qualities, a generous cockpit for my cameras, and great cargo capacity. Like an old full-size Kelty frame backpack, these first Northwest kayaks are comfortable, stable, high-volume boats, good for cruising the protected waters of Puget Sound and British Columbia's Georgia Strait.

Chart #18448, Puget Sound South Part, scale 1:80,000 (or: 1 foot on the chart = 13.5 nautical miles on the Sound) is a huge sheet of paper folded and refolded to display my first day's route along the southwestern edge of the South Sound. From Budd Inlet I planned to cross Dana Passage, paddle past Hope Island and, keeping to the western shore of Squaxin Island, travel north through Pickering Passage to Jarrell Cove on the very north end of Hartstene Island. Sixteen miles: a strong day for the average paddler, since it would involve paddling against the tide and against the wind for the better part of the journey. I resecured my chart case, put on my sunglasses, pushed up my sleeves, and tightened my spray skirt. Then I left Budd Inlet and Olympia behind.

The rhythm of a crossing is set by the steady draw-and-push of the paddle. Draw-and-push: my hands not closed over the paddle shaft but open like a hook, like an orangutan swinging from vine to vine. Draw-and-push: the water so close my whole being is conscious of it. The wave at my bow was just audible above the background sounds of a cool morning, a riffled surface. Less than a mile and a half before I reached the south end of Squaxin Island, I crossed the wake of a small ketch under auxiliary power running with the tide, the only other boat in sight. I watched her disappear toward Tacoma, knowing I was warmer than her bundled skipper as I continued my steady labor, the exercise heating the boat beneath my spray skirt. Draw-and-push: I felt loose and comfortable, my attentions now focused on the surprise appearance of a marbled murrelet that surfaced off my bow, flared its wings, and dove to safety.

Beyond the puddle left by the vanished murrelet, a sudden gust of wind—what sailors call a "cat's paw"—moved toward me. I watched the water roughen and turn a blue-black color. Then, as the wind hit, I leaned into it to counteract the force. In a moment it was gone, but more would come. That is the way of cat's paws: they signal a rising wind. I changed course accordingly, leaving the wind and the main channel to beachcomb the coast of Squaxin Island, enjoying the lift where the wind meets the land.

Around the midpoint of the four-mile-long south shore of Squaxin lies Hope Island, a Washington State Marine Park, with a fine shell beach on its southern shore. I had been staring at this particular beach for quite some time, hoping to go ashore there for lunch. But Hope is at the center of the tidal energy flowing into Squaxin Passage from four inlets, so currents off this beach are among the most complex in the Sound. The tide can

The ubiquitous bird of the Sound, a great blue heron (Ardea herodias), *in Dana Passage.*

rush around Hope Island so fast that you find yourself paddling in place. Realizing my predicament, I slowly closed the gap between Squaxin Island's Potlatch Point and the north shore of Hope, my two landmarks. Suddenly I shot forward as I crossed the eddyline that separates the ebb flow from the protected water in the lee of the island. As the wind dropped away, the sun's warmth hit me full force. I popped my spray skirt and paddled toward shore in pleasant anticipation of lunch.

The beach's lone inhabitant, a great blue heron, politely moved down the shore with nary a squawk as I grounded in the shallows. The salt grass was verdant, the beach a mix of cobble, pebble, and shell with a concentration of crushed clamshells too high to have occurred naturally. I could only assume I was not the first person to have enjoyed lunch here. Though too small to have supported a village, Hope Island may have been a summer gathering site for one of the many small tribes of the South Sound Coast Salish people: the Skwakwksin or Skwaks-namish of upper Case Inlet, the S'Hotleemamish of southern Case Inlet, the Sahehwamish of Hammersley Inlet, the Sawamish of Totten Inlet, the Skwai-sitl of Eld Inlet, the Stehtsasamish of Budd Inlet, or the Nusehtsatl of Henderson Inlet. All were within a few canoe-miles of here.

Once ashore, I set my wooden plate on a bed of shells and rummaged through the lunch bag for the makings of two peanut butter and raspberry jam sandwiches and a still-cool pale ale. My Coast Salish predecessors here would have lunched on baked fern-root flour and fish eggs with dried herring, bones and all.

As I cleared Hope Island, I wondered how well the Coast Salish in their western red cedar canoes had handled these tricky waters. This pass must have been intimately known to the experienced Native paddlers, and perhaps it served as a training ground for the younger Salish as well. It would be training enough for me as I stopped just north of Hope to glean what I could from the chart. Ahead, the outflow from ten-mile-long Hammersley Inlet and eight-mile-long Totten Inlet converge, swirl, and bounce off Squaxin, some of the flow being forced north up Pickering Passage, the rest struggling to pass Hope Island. Suddenly I looked up and saw that the current was carrying me swiftly backward, so I set aside the chart and paddled forward to a point where I could safely restudy my position. The chart showed Totten's mouth to be broad and deep (fourteen fathoms, or eighty-four feet), while Hammersley's is less than an eighth of a mile wide and

A north breeze bends salt grasses and brings the smell of oysters to the Hope Island beach site.

only twelve feet deep at low tide. Hammersley boasts currents that far exceed Totten's. Known in the Chinook jargon of the 1850s as "Big Skookum" or "big strong," the inlet's currents move at times in excess of five knots. I stowed the chart and, keeping a light grip on the paddle shaft, began to glide across Totten's flow to where it meets Hammersley's in the daily chaos of the South Pickering Passage tide rip.

A tide rip is alive—a moving, surging riot of water. There are boils welling up, eddylines of opposing currents colliding, whirlpools appearing and disappearing, standing waves marking submarine reefs, and noise—a deep-throated hum and thrash of water. When Totten's current swept me into the stronger tongue from Hammersley Inlet, my bow wrenched around, first one way and then another, as I entered the confluence. Moving from boil to boil, I paddled north as the ebb took me east. Beside me, whirlpools made a sucking sound as they trapped air and took it beneath the surface. Between two boils, I misstroked. Reaching out with the flat of my paddle, I slapped the water to brace the kayak and regain my balance. A series of greasy waves—short, steep, and larger than the rest—signaled a border eddy and I dipped through, taking water over the bow and some spray in my face. Minutes later, spit out of the main current, I checked the shore for my bearings. Sure enough, Hammersley's jet of current had bounced off Squaxin and split apart, leaving me to ride the lesser current north through Pickering Passage. I was right where I wanted to be, and I proceeded to set a pace for the final five miles.

Pickering Passage, an eight-mile-long, half-mile-wide channel that separates Squaxin and Hartstene Islands from the mainland of the Olympic Peninsula, was named after Charles Pickering, the ethnographer on the U.S. Exploration Expedition of 1838 to 1842. Commanded by Lieutenant Charles Wilkes, the expedition surveyed Puget Sound and the San Juans throughout the spring and summer of 1841, naming and renaming every feature they came in contact with, in order to claim the territory and erase the earlier hold of the Spanish and British explorers. Over two hundred names stuck, among them Hope, Hammersley, Totten, and Hartstene. Squaxin got its name in 1854 when the Medicine Creek treaty was signed. Described by Thomas T. Waterman in his study of

A bald eagle (Haliaeetus leucocephalus), *throat coated in oil, stares into an uncertain future on Squaxin Island.*

Coast Salish place names, *Puget Sound Geography*, as "scantily wooded and rather useless," Squaxin became the least desirable reservation of the South Sound as American settlers took control of the Salish country. Waterman noted that in the namesake tribe's language, Skwaks-namish means "alone people."

I passed Squaxin's northern point, named Salmon Point by Wilkes and *Y'lb nx* by the Skwaks-namish after a supernatural power who brings herring. On up the passage, every cove, bluff, and islet had a Native name far more descriptive than the one given it by the 1841 expedition: "wild goose" for a low promontory on Squaxin, "oak trees" for a rise on Hartstene, "where there are cranes" for an island on my right just off Pickering's eastern shore. I stayed to that side, passing high banks with madrona hanging on the edge, roots exposed.

It was 3 P.M. when I crossed the channel as it bent eastward; sensing the current falling away and reversing, I aimed for the beach. As I followed it, I saw the exposed tide bank explode with clam squirts. I counted a hundred strokes, then two hundred, playing mental games to ease the final leg to my first campsite.

Jarrell Cove, my destination, was reputed to be a beautiful little two-armed inlet at the north end of Hartstene Island. The Skwaks-namish knew it as *DE'xudExwl*. The name means "hunting canoes," for this cove was "a place where good cedar timber could be found for the manufacture of canoes," according to *Puget Sound Geography*. As I turned into the narrow confines of the bay, I felt pleased at the meeting of canoe and kayak cultures a century apart.

The Cascadia Marine Trail guidebook led me toward a campsite at the north end of a narrow beach on the eastern shore, where I got out of the cockpit and hung my boots over the side as I glided ashore. On the bank beside a path leading up to the campsite, I saw a sturdy post topped by a small brown sign with the silhouette of a kayaker painted on it. I was on the Trail.

> ### SUPPLIES
>
> *In my kayak I packed food for ten days, two bottles of red wine, and a full kitchen that included two nesting pots, a white-gas stove, a large coffee filter, a garlic press, a pepper grinder, a cherished "Banks Fry-Bake" Dutch oven, and a couple of wooden plates that double as cutting boards. My small library included* Birds of North America; Trees, Shrubs, and Flowers to Know in British Columbia; Marine Wildlife of Puget Sound, the San Juans, and the Strait of Georgia; *H.A. Rey's* The Stars; *and two Aubrey-Maturin novels by Patrick O'Brian. I had a three-man tent, my headlamp, a Therm-a-Rest pad, a summer sleeping bag with flannel liner, a VHF ICOM radio for weather reports and emergencies, and a life jacket, rescue float, flares, pump, and sponge. Strapped to the deck in a giant ziplock bag were my compass, tide book, current tables, and charts.*

The view from camp at the Jarrell Cove trail site.

The next morning my stove wouldn't work. Grumbling, oblivious to the makings of a fine day, I stripped the assembly, suspecting a clogged fuel line. With the jet cleared, it lighted, sputtered, and ran. I too lightened up, sputtered, and ran—boiled the water, filtered the coffee, and took note of my surroundings. The camp at Jarrell Cove was not pretty. The tent and communal area, recently carved from a slope once covered in

THE PATHWAYS OF KINGFISHERS

bracken fern and timber, smelled of raw earth. At its center, a picnic table stood chained to the firmament. But given the state marine park's limited shoreline, this site's location—away from the landbound campers and the toilets—made it a model trail site.

Where once Salish paddlers and European explorers camped when and where weather and convenience dictated, today there simply are no unclaimed beaches left. We Washington Water Trails volunteers relied upon the magnanimity of the Washington State Marine Parks, the state Department of Natural Resources, and local governments for the beginnings of a trail network. As I broke camp and loaded Boato, I told myself that however ungainly the Cascadia Marine Trail seemed now, in time it would grow into its own. Once I got back on the water and pointed northeast up the last of Pickering Passage, I began to see the Trail as one of many—some forgotten, others fresh, one overlaying the other like late summer salt grass, a link to understanding this sea between the mountains.

Boato tucked in atop the beach berm as
evening comes to Anderson Island.

Beneath these waters is the greatest of trails: the floor of the Sound itself, a striated seascape of basin, sill, and fjord left raw and desolate in the melting retreat of the great Pleistocene glaciers. The returning sea invaded the lowlands, transporting the larvae of urchins, sea stars, and oysters via its tidal pathways. The herring and salmon in search of spawning redds pioneered the Sound's hereditary anadromous migration routes. Then for perhaps 8,000 years the Salish paddled its pathways, in time crossing wakes with European seafarers like Manuel Quimper, George Vancouver, and Charles Wilkes, who in turn emboldened the first pioneers. Pioneer settlement brought the steamboats, paddle wheels thrashing, that raced up and down these channels. World trade attracted 50,000-gross-ton container ships on newly established traffic lanes to the growing port cities; powerboats, sailboats, or kayaks went everywhere else, crossing and recrossing all the waterways of the Sound. As I entered Case Inlet, I was haunted by these innumerable voyagers, so many of whom had passed right through this point. It was as if I were paddling with the phantoms of an invisible history, rich and unknown.

The fourteen-mile-long Key Peninsula that separates Case and Carr Inlets lay two miles distant, shrouded by traveling clouds. As I cleared the point the locals call "the rock" because of its prominent glacial erratic, little Stretch Island, known by the Skwaks-namish as a summer gathering site for butter clams, came into view. I headed toward its south-facing beach and landed amid clam squirts. The ex-Confederate bachelor soldier Lambert Evans may have first set foot on Stretch Island here in 1872. The gently sloping meadow above the beach would have been ideal for the collection of vine cuttings he had brought. He paid cash for the land to raise grapes and encouraged his quickly arriving neighbors to do the same.

By 1889 the settlement on and opposite Stretch Island had become known as the Detroit Townsite, with a population of 300. A hotel was begun but never finished. The railroad was expected but never came. An ambitious project to connect Detroit by water with nearby Hood Canal never left the drawing board. After too much mail ended up in

MOSQUITO FLEET MUSEUM

Today the warehouse of the old Saint Charles winery on Stretch Island houses the little-known Puget Sound Museum. Charles "Bill" Somers—founder, curator, guide, and onetime deckhand on the old steamer Hayak—walked me through this museum, a place now solely devoted to his passion for and memory of steamboats. Room after room is filled with oak-spoked ship's wheels, brass bells, and foghorn bladders (which look like hand-held bellows). Gilt nameboards that once graced pilot houses now decorate the walls. A hundred models of paddle wheelers, side-wheelers, and propeller-driven steamers lie everywhere, folk masterpieces of a time when the Sound was the only highway and the steamers presented a rare moment of grace and elegance in a pioneer setting.

From brig-rigged vessels of discovery to stay-sailed lumber ships, wind power ruled the Sound from the 1780s to the 1930s.

Detroit, Michigan, the residents renamed the town Grapeview for what Lambert Evans had begun with his cuttings. (Mail then began to show up in Grandview, Washington.) Evans's insistence that his neighbors plant vineyards paid off; by 1938 Grapeview had the largest winery in the state. In 1965, however, the Saint Charles winery crushed its last grape. Grapeview's metropolitan hopes, like those of its neighbors Allyn, Stadium, Vaughn, and Clifton, dissolved in the backwaters of the South Sound.

I spent the night above the Stretch Island beach in Bill Somers's 1890s farmhouse and woke to a quilt-cold morning, brief sunlight, and low-tide mud. I carried the empty kayak, the coaming balanced on my shoulder, a hundred yards to the incoming tide and then ferried the gear. It was to be a twelve-mile day, one on which I would follow the track the local steamboats would have taken down Sound.

The South Sound is a network of shallow inlets and interconnecting passages, the most convoluted shoreline in the entire Puget Sound, with almost 30 percent of the Sound's total shoreline but only 10 percent of its surface area. That morning I was faced with a four-mile diagonal crossing of the open water between Case Inlet and Key Peninsula. From the moment I cleared the south point of Stretch Island, I met a steady crosswind and rain blurring the southwest horizon. The short sharp seas began to build, and the rain worked slantwise against the side of my face.

It was a relief to tuck up against the protected eastern shore of Herron Island where, on a similar afternoon in May 1792, Peter Puget, second officer aboard Captain George Vancouver's HMS *Discovery*, had also sought protection. Puget and his men raised a tarp of sail canvas. I was wearing a hooded Gore-Tex paddling jacket layered over my spray skirt, a pile pullover, and a polypropylene top. To keep the rest of me warm, I relied on coated nylon rain pants over a pair of shorts. The only cotton was a baseball cap I wore so the water wouldn't drip off my nose. But in a rain like this (a truly pernicious sort of rain), I was neither waterproof nor dry. So I began to sing.

I have memorized only one complete song in my life ("Willing" by Lowell George),

Bill Somers holds one of his many steamship models from the Puget Sound Museum, Stretch Island.

and though I'm not tone-deaf, my singing voice is at its best one or two octaves offshore. But I needed company out there, so I made up songs. Keeping time to my stroke and the waves that beat spray up and over my head, I sang out my lyrics and kept to the rhythms like a mallet-fisted cadence keeper aboard an ancient galley.

So entertained, I paddled through the weather to the next site on the Trail: Joemma Beach State Park (until recently known as RFK Recreation Site). At midpoint in the day's journey, six miles out from Stretch Island, I dried out

Skipping rocks and pursuing elusive tans: beachgoers at Joemma Beach State Park.

beneath a picnic shelter near an open bluff overlook. There were four tent sites directly behind me, secluded, well situated, and vacant. Fighting off crows, I settled in for a simple lunch and watched the people-who-deny-rain paying homage to the beach: kids endlessly skipping rocks, a sloop's crew tying their boat at the public dock, the captain coming ashore with the ship's dog. Four adults were hunched on the dock's floats, checking and rechecking their baited crab traps. Some people just drove down to the fenced cliff edge and, without leaving their cars, looked out through steaming windows at the clouds breaking, the waters of Case Inlet silver with the reappearing sun.

By the time I reached my next destination, Anderson Island, the day looked and felt different—blue sky, bright sun, a workable wind. Golden light penetrated deep into the fir and hemlock forest, illuminating the trees and making them glow, setting the red-barked madronas' limbs ablaze with color. Closing with the beach, I continued along the shore, spooking a belted kingfisher that moved noisily ahead, perched, and, as I neared again, screeched away. Only a dislodged great blue heron with its old man's disdainful alarm—"*Arahhh, Arahhh, Arhhh, Ahh!*"—can make you feel more guilty for intruding. A hundred yards ahead, the kingfisher veered into a small bay. I checked the trail guidebook and, seeing that we were to be neighbors, veered in behind him.

The trail site was situated on a beautiful baymouth bar with no sign or announcement of the Cascadia Marine Trail. I hauled Boato across a tideline littered with thousands of sand dollars. Above the berm and the lagoon beyond, there were no houses, no people. It looked to be as pristine and beautiful as it might have been in Puget's time. (He camped on Anderson in Oro Bay, again in thunder, lightning, and rain. Poor guy: No one told him about Puget Sound in May.) I found a windless pocket behind a drift log and set up the kitchen. I wouldn't even bother with a tent.

I was here by the grace of the residents of Anderson Island, for this is a different sort of trail site, not part of the state lands. Anderson was one of the first sites granted by a local island community; Washington Water Trails members are permitted to stay overnight here after reserving it with the association. With careful use and good behavior on the part of paddlers, Washington Water Trails hopes to retain its welcome by the islanders, so its members may continue to share what is actually the local park. As I contemplated dinner, an island resident appeared, hop-skipping across the lagoon on a path of drift logs to reach the beach. We nodded hello and returned to our own worlds. By nightfall six separate parties, both couples and solitary beach walkers, had quietly passed by my camp.

To anyone who sea kayaks, dinnertime means more than just eating. It means celebrating the end of the daily fussing-about (what I call knick-

Sand dollars (Dendraster excentricus) *display their sea-star lineage with five-rayed patterns.*

knacking). From the moment I landed, I had a long list of tasks to complete: secure the boat, raise the tarp, site the stove, discover the ants, resite the stove, chop vegetables, keep the cameras and film out of the sun. Now, facing a just-set sun, I leaned back on a smooth beach log, with way too much spaghetti on my plate, and took a sip of red wine. The South Sound lay flat calm. Not a boat to be seen, and nary a sound. Over my left shoulder the kingfisher darted into the lagoon and returned to his perch with a wriggling silver catch. I raised my cup in salute and we both settled in for a meal.

Gulls, seals, salmon, and fishers of all kinds converge on a herring ball.

Mount Rainier is forty-eight miles from the southwest corner of Anderson Island; nonetheless, I had to tilt my head back as the mountain came into view. A stratovolcano of layered lava, pumice, and ash, at 14,411 feet it is the reigning physical feature of the region. From its snowcapped flanks, freshets turn to streams and streams to rivers: the Nisqually, the Puyallup, the White, and the Carbon—all of which meet the Sound and bring it their silt and salmon smolts. About two miles off my kayak's bow, the Nisqually meets the Sound in a meandering estuary that by a miracle of early environmental activism (credit the Audubon Society's Hazel Wolf) has been preserved as a refuge. The Nisqually Delta is considered the most pristine of the Sound's remaining estuaries, and for now its immediate surroundings are free of development as well. I was looking at one of the last remaining strips of wilderness shore left in Puget Sound.

When I paddled away from Nisqually Reach into the heart of the South Sound, my route became a slalom course: steering from the east side of Anderson, crossing Balch Passage to the west side of McNeil Island, from McNeil crossing Pitt Passage to the east of the Key Peninsula, and then making a long crossing of Carr Inlet to Kopachuck State Park. The day was marked by opposing currents, headwinds, and lots of beach hugging to avoid it all. At times I'd creep by strings of summer homes built gable-to-eve wherever the high bluffs relaxed to level beachfront. Close inshore, fighting the tide within feet of fish float–decorated decks and crumbling seawalls, I could mark my progress in inches.

In Balch Passage I began noticing salmon fry swimming beside me just as I met a twelve-foot outboard carrying two marine biologists counting—salmon fry. When I asked how the salmon were doing they replied, "Fewer," and returned to their tabulating.

By my fourth day on the South Sound I had begun to realize that these shores were the least disturbed or developed part of the Cascadia Marine Trail. Far from population centers, it is an isolated dead end for boaters and hard to get to by car. The summer houses I had passed by were just that—not the 5,000-square-foot retirement homes of the 1990s but cottages from the first decades of the century. There were no kayakers, few boaters, no jets overhead or submarines underneath. Aside from Bill Somers's hospitality and a few encounters at Joemma Beach and Jarrell Cove, I had been entirely in the company of nature.

Every mile or so, a copse of alder had recently crashed to the beach from the high bluffs. Beneath them a talus of glacial clay and sand, eroding from tide and wind action, was being transported elsewhere: to sustain a beach, to close off a bay, to constantly change the way things are done around here. On the water and in the air came a constant stream of marine birds: coots, grebes, pigeon guillemots, herons, and eagles. I was cir-cled by cormorants and inspected by western gulls. Harbor seals sniffed my passing; herring bit the surface, then flashed away at my shadow. A lame fox searching the tideline for food noticed me and trotted to a safe midcliff vantage to casually wash itself, one eye cocked on my progress.

And it was progress—cold, wet progress—that eventually brought me to Kopachuck State Park. I paddled along the treed shore until I spotted the state park boundary fence. And though I couldn't see a trail-site sign, I made my landfall and splashed ashore. The six-mile crossing of Carr Inlet had been long and choppy, with a current to slow me and a series of squalls that caused me to question my judgment. My body buzzed from the energy expended; my hands were like claws.

How to see a harbor seal (Phoca vitulena) *from a kayak? Paddle upwind backward.*

Crossing to Hartstene Island between Case Inlet and Pickering Passage.

Using some massive roots as footholds, I clambered up an undercut bank and at the top found the marine trail campsite sign, a picnic table, and a set of tent spots in a secluded forest setting. In no time I had heaped my gear on the table, draped my clothes to dry on the water-trail sign, and put water on to boil for some Earl Grey tea.

The sun came out in the final hours of the day, dappling the camp and enlivening the forest birds as they sang and scruffed about in the understory. I walked through the maple and hemlock and back down to the beach. The sun lay straight across the head of the inlet, with just a bit of the Olympic Mountains visible through rent clouds. In the trees behind me, a Swainson's thrush began its evening song.

On the morning of the fifth day, I awoke to forest sounds. Squirrels were everywhere—including on the picnic table. Robins, wrens, and a pair of rufous-sided towhees all flitted from perch to ground to perch. I lay in my tent watching, listening, and procrastinating. Suddenly the forest went on alert: the squirrels vamoosed, the morning songs ceased. It was as if time had stopped. Then I heard fast, running feet and saw a blaze of movement through the green growth. Two dogs in the heat of the hunt, for a moment as wild as dingoes, skidded into camp, panting, heaving, alive. It was like a scene from *Watership Down*. Nothing moved. No sound, no calls. All at once a man appeared, offered profuse apologies for the disturbance, and corralled "Mandy" and "Shadow." Then the briefly suburban forest returned to silence.

I settled back into my sleeping bag and checked the tidebook. Last night's "high-high," the higher of the two high tides of the day, had been a grand 15.0 feet. By 9:40 A.M. this fifteen feet of standing water 143 miles square would have churned through the Tacoma Narrows, which was my destination that day. Then it would reverse and

HALCYON DAYS

"In ancient times of myths and fables, kingfishers or halcyons were said to build a floating nest on the sea, and to possess some mysterious power that calmed the troubled waves while the eggs were hatching and the young birds were being reared, hence the term 'halcyon days,' meaning days of fair weather."
—Neltje Blanchan, *Bird Neighbors*

The eggs of Ceryle alcyon, *the belted kingfisher, hatch around the second week of June, signaling the beginning of good weather in the Puget Sound region. Featherless balls with legs and beaks, the chicks are each fed the equivalent of 8.3 Coho salmon fingerlings per day before they're fully fledged in twenty-seven to twenty-nine days. Once they have learned to fish—the mother catches, maims, and returns a small fish to the water, and then coaxes her young in after it—they may stay in the area or wander. The mature kingfisher has a fierce instinct for territoriality and is capable of giving chase to interlopers at roughly 36 miles an hour.*

regather strength, flowing past Vashon Island and Tacoma, almost twelve feet of it flooding back through the Narrows, vibrating the bridge that spans the mile-wide channel. By 4:08 in the afternoon it would be my turn; after yesterday's current and squalls, I wanted a ride.

Waiting for the ebb tide, I dawdled, loafed, applied sunscreen, and took an early lunch. When I finally shoved off and had Fox Island to larboard and the Key Peninsula to starboard, I took out my trusty Patrick O'Brian. To read whenever I liked was a particular pleasure; to read in the kayak was something of a science. I propped a driftwood stick upright on my foredeck as a sort of crude sundial. Then, as long as the stick's

Semi-appropriate use of a Cascadia Marine Trail sign, Kopachuck State Park.

shadow stayed stationary, I could read about the eighteenth-century peccadillos of Jack Aubrey and the pale-eyed intrigue of Dr. Maturin without paying attention to where I was going. On down Hale Passage I rode the last of the morning ebb while deep in my book. When my attention flagged enough to cause me to look up, I saw that I was afloat in Wollochet Bay.

Peter Puget had explored here: "We found a Small Cove at the head of which were a Party of Seventeen to Eighteen Indians in temporary Habitations drying Clams Fish &c which they readily parted with for Buttons Trinkets &c they did not appear the least alarmed at our Approach." Today Wollochet (Coast Salish for either "squirting clams" or "cut throat") is suffering its fourth wave of European settlement. Now boasting mega-waterfront houses, it's a bedroom community of Tacoma. The pioneers' houses of the 1870s and 1880s have disappeared, and the summer homes of the 1920s have all but vanished as well. Now even the quite substantial postwar waterfront houses are being torn down and replaced by monuments to successful car dealerships. It was an awesome display of mortgages. The final indignity came when I paddled past a group of kids drifting in a ski-boat and one of them yelled, "Go find a river." I paddled off as the tide gathered like a river into the Narrows, leaving the South Sound behind.

The "Doc" Weathers trail site is at the mouth of a small ravine, one of the few breaks in the high bluffs that characterize the Tacoma Narrows. The ravine's outwash meets the Sound in a broken line of driftwood and a sand beach, dominated by the graceful silhouette of the Tacoma Narrows Bridge. Above the drift logs I saw a ranch-style house with a weed-choked concrete deck and no sign of life. This onetime home of

TO CAPTURE A SAILOR'S HEART

"Doc" Weathers and his family would soon be part of a new Pierce County Park which, once improvements were made, would also include a water-trail site. It just wasn't here yet. I was trespassing.

I hunkered down with my headlamp and peered at the chart, measuring tomorrow's miles and consulting the tide table to figure out my timing. As a Foss tug rumbled by, bucking the evening ebb, I set my alarm for a cruel 4:15 A.M. Salmon fishermen drifted in the opposite direction, their cigarettes glowing, as I rolled out my sleeping bag. And a heron, more shadow than reality, glided noiselessly over me as I fell asleep.

At this latitude, in this year, the earliest sunrise occurs on June 12 at 5 A.M. I raced it, paddling into the coolness of the morning with a current that pulled me rapidly toward the Narrows Bridge, the orange-to-yellow dawn rising through its support cables. I steered to the north bastion, the highway some 160 feet above, the

*Tailing the MV Sea-Land Kodiak
into Commencement Bay, Tacoma.*

bridge humming with the first of the Monday traffic between Tacoma and the Kitsap Peninsula.

How smug I felt passing beneath the rumble and radio of the on-the-way-to-work world! With a hundred miles of paddling beneath my keel I lived in a different reality, my slow-paced paddle, nightly campsites, and random sightings of wildlife clashing with this sudden stream of traffic. Just then, part of a tree spinning erratically in the boils rafted up beside me. I fended it off and stroked away toward the opposite shore.

On both sides of the Narrows the shore rears up to three and four hundred feet in a sweeping bend to the north. The alders and maples cloaking the palisades, coupled with the fast-moving current, gave me the illusion of paddling a river—the Hudson maybe, near West Point. On the south bank a shoreside community known as Salmon Beach loomed up in the shade of sunrise. Nestled on pilings beneath the bluffs stands a half-mile-long string of cottages, no doubt the bane of the Pierce County building department. Modest to tiny multi-leveled, multi-windowed structures, they are festooned with wind chimes, god's eyes, and houseplants and are accessible only by boat or by a series of wooden staircases winding down the hillside. I had stumbled upon the shangri-la of waterfront dreams.

These are the homes of those who would rather gamble with the fragile geology above them than forsake their on-the-edge-of-the-Sound lifestyle; in fact, I could see where one home had recently been destroyed by a mud slide. I found this community unnerving but attractive nonetheless: this was waterfront property I could afford. Wondering

The Tacoma Narrows Bridge at dawn; the center span is 2,595 feet long and 180 feet high.

A landslide destroyed this Salmon Beach home in the Narrows.

about the lives lived here, imagining the great summer sunsets enjoyed by the fortunate if temporary residents, and noticing that no one was up and about yet, I drifted toward Point Defiance and the sun.

Beneath Point Defiance on Commencement Bay, salmon fishermen in ones and twos trolled in a brilliant corn-yellow light. In the distance, beyond the Point Defiance–Vashon Island ferry, the high-rises of Tacoma loomed, Mount Rainier lording over it all. I pulled out my camera and tried to frame the scene, letting my kayak wander with the morning's energy.

Suddenly I heard a shout. One of the fishermen had a fish on. He was fighting what turned out to be an eight-pound king salmon, and his happiness was evident as I drifted by.

It was decision time. I sat in the middle of the bay and rechecked the tidebook. If I paddled to Tacoma and explored its harbor, waterways, and bustling container port, I would add several hours and miles to my day. By late morning the turn of the tide would make the crossing to Vashon a tough one, and it would stay tough for six hours. Reluctantly I turned and aimed for Quartermaster Harbor in company with the Vashon-bound ferry.

Ernie Perlath used a chrome-and-white flasher with a green "hoochie" to catch his eight-pound king.

There were four quartermasters aboard the sloop of war *Vincennes* in May 1841 when the U.S. Exploration Expedition charted Vashon Island. They were seasoned and skilled navy men in charge of the ship's helm, compass, and signals. Their commander, Charles Wilkes, named the points of the island—Neill, Robinson, Dalco, and Beal—in their honor. Then, in a further acknowledgment of their collective value in an era when sailors "before the mast" rarely received such permanent recognition, Wilkes named Vashon's only harbor "Quarter Masters Harbour." At least one of these sailors most likely assisted in surveying this promising anchorage.

Using longboats, they marked their progress by lead-line and

triangulation, crossing the entrance from Neill Point to Manzanita as they took sound-ings for their charts. One hundred and fifty-five years later I crossed their track and entered the long, slender harbor that bears their name. Quartermaster Harbor, as it is known today, is well protected from winter winds, with depths sufficient to anchor yet shallow enough to accept piers. By the 1890s, men like the Manson brothers and John Martinolich would begin driving piles and building piers, dry docks, and shipyards to ring the bays. By the turn of the century there were brickyards, a codfish packing plant, a box plant, canneries, and of course sawmills fronting the Quartermaster shore. Steamboats raced in to unload new workers, then loaded fresh berries and bolts of shakes and raced out again, bow waves rising. Towns platted themselves up the stump-riddled hills: Burton, Dockton, Quartermaster, and Portage. And near the crest of West Hill, Vashon College stood in lone splendor amid the remaining tall timber. With its substan-tial Victorian buildings, at the time it could accommodate more students than any other campus in the state.

As I paddled past the wavering pilings that once anchored this bustling harbor's heyday, I could only imagine the four- and five-masted lumber schooners, hulls three hundred feet long, being built on the ways: the thock of mallets and the scream of saws. Bands of smoke from the cedar kilns and steamboat stacks would have turned the harbor's still air blue and sweet-sharp. Above it all Homer and Herodotus would have reigned supreme at the college, whose curriculum included Oratory, Rhetoric, Spherical Trigonometry, and Use of the Typewriter.

After World War I the mainland's railroads, highways, cities, and universities sucked the industry and the aspirations from Vashon. The timber was gone, the college had burned and was never rebuilt, the shipyards had moved or scaled down to building fishing boats. Quartermaster Harbor, Vashon Island, and adjoining Maury Island fell into the hands of the real-estate developers.

The Summer People, Maury Island historian Howard Lynn called them. They came from their homes in Tacoma and Seattle on the steamers and ferries to beach cottages that sold for $1,200 (with furniture and a boat!). They moved into housing developments named Rosehill, Harbor Heights, Indian Point, Magnolia Beach,

California sea lions (Zalophus californianus) *ride a midchannel buoy off Maury Island.*

Sailboats at anchor off Burton, with the Cascade Range in the distance.

and Manzanita, each creating a new community clustered along the beach or hidden in the returning forest, now home to a fourth generation.

I twisted and turned with the course of the harbor, still lined with these beach bungalows. To my eye, little had changed since the 1920s. True, the island was becoming something of a "bedroom community" of Tacoma and Seattle; nonetheless, the money and extravagance I'd witnessed in Wollochet Bay had not come to Quartermaster or to Vashon's one remaining town, Burton. The business district of Burton had once climbed the hill to Vashon College, and only now was the "campus" experiencing the infill of new houses.

I tethered Boato at the marina and walked into town. Burton has a fine presence of the sea, like the smallest of the coastal towns north of Portland, Maine. There is a classic, pioneer-scale American Baptist church built in 1897 as well as a false-fronted, sleeping dog–decorated Harbor Mercantile (1908). Despite Burton's diminished glory, the town has retained its post office, next door to which a new business, Internet Web Services (www.vashon.com), seems poised to take it away. Across the street, between the boxy Masonic Hall and Don's Shell Station, I saw yet another sign of progress: the Cafe Nautica, which everybody calls the Burton Espresso Stand. It was there that I ran into Danny O'Keefe.

Over a couple of double-tall split-skinny extra-hot hold-foam lattes, we shared the fine morning sunlight while Danny's dog, Keisha, cadged for a handout. I knew Danny from his music-making and his fondness for a Seattle tavern I liked, the Virginia Inn. He and his partner, occupational therapist Laurie Hare, had left Los Angeles for Vashon "the day John Lennon died."

They bought a Victorian house, built before records were kept, that faces south across the site of the old campus. Laurie established her professional practice, while Danny continued to write music and perform it on tour off-island. I had always been

THE MAKING OF A TRAIL SITE

On a sunny May afternoon in 1996, nearly a hundred people gathered to celebrate the culmination of a four-year effort to make the "Doc" Weathers property on the north side of the Tacoma Narrows a park and Cascadia Marine Trail campsite. The park was initially proposed by the Peninsula Heritage Land Trust. The Trust for Public Lands did the negotiating, and the County Conservation Futures, the Washington Wildlife and Recreation Program, and the federal Land and Water Conservation Fund paid for the property. Championed in particular by Pierce County councilwoman Karen Biskey and Jon Ortgiesen of Pierce County Parks and Recreation, the "Doc" Weathers site is an example of the intricate and expanding network of cooperation between agencies required to create a public recreation area. With this park and campsite at the Narrows, a key piece of the Cascadia Marine Trail fell into place: not only is it in the middle of a 16-mile gap, it is a jumping-off point to both the South Sound and points north.

The living room of Danny O'Keefe and Laurie Hare's Vashon Island home.

susceptible to the lure of an island, of a water-ringed creative life, and Danny's life, his pace, his world appealed to me greatly. But after sixteen years here, Danny was clearly worried about the changing character of the island. "The problem with people moving into an area that's rural," he says, "is that after a while a certain density is reached and then it's not rural any longer. The island is really close to that threshold now. Once you reach that threshold, then privacy becomes a big deal again." Ironically, he's not alone in his concern. The most recent proposal by the state Department of Transportation to build a bridge linking the mainland to Vashon brought 2,000 heavily anti-bridge Vashonites to the high school. (Vashon's population is 9,309.)

Maury Island, in Charles Wilkes's day, was a separate island only at high tide. Today the two islands are joined by about three hundred feet of road, houses, and a general store/lending library/local museum. The store (and the isthmus itself) is called Portage, which was what I had to do rather than circumpaddle Maury Island. I beached the kayak on firm mud wreathed in bright green sea lettuce and extricated all my gear.

Crossing the portage at Portage, Vashon Island.

In three loads I carried it to the eastern beach known as Tramp Harbor. Then came the boat. Using a wadded T-shirt as a pad, I hoisted the *Eugene Odum* on my shoulder and marched down the road, arousing mild curiosity among passing motorists.

I knew I was on the trail of the Salish canoes. They had to have used this passage, knowing they'd save three miles, timing their day to make high water. The S'Homamish of Gig Harbor (the Narrows) may have come this way,

staying close inshore on a north wind, scaring the *sxatc* (sole) and *sxwádi* (bullhead) beneath their keels. So too the Puyallups from villages near Tacoma came ashore on Vashon to hunt for berry and root patches that lay inland. Many sources speak of a time before the Europeans when the feared Haida raided south from the five-hundred-mile-distant Queen Charlottes—they must have paddled stealthily along this villageless shore, but the Salish knew of their coming, and ambushed and defeated them at what is now Portage.

Twilight camp, the Winghaven site, Vashon Island.

Five and a half miles north of Portage, not far from the dock for the Seattle ferry, I found the Cascadia Marine Trail site known as Winghaven. It is set in a ravine that cuts into a three-hundred-foot-high cliff and sloping hillside. I had kayaked to Winghaven the previous summer, before it had identifying signage. I had paddled back and forth along a bay treed in alder and firs: no site. Passing a substantial seawall capped with a crenellated walk, a fine lawn, and rhododendrons as big as trucks, I'd felt certain this million-dollar piece of property couldn't be the trail site. Seeing no evidence of recent trail-site building and unwilling to trespass, I'd paddled on to Lisabeula, a real park—an established, signed site with an actual picnic table. (The Lisabeula trail site is on Vashon's western shore, toward the southern end of Colvos Passage.) A few weeks later the Washington Water Trails volunteers, along with employees of the corporate sponsors, returned to dedicate the Winghaven site after dumping tons of fill to shore the seawall, doing concrete work on the grand staircase to the beach, and spending days hacking back the blackberry vines and nettles. Now this King County property is a Vashon Island park.

This time I spied the seawall long before anything else on this sparsely developed shore, and then I saw the unmistakable little kayak sign that signifies a trail site, right at the stairway to the lawn. It was eerie: the concrete lions, the well-mowed lawn, the space for a mansion but no sign of one. I felt as if I'd become an element in a painting by Magritte—the campsite of the gods, formal outdoor wear required. But the picnic table in the center of the greensward brought me back to the reality of wet polypro. I unceremoniously draped the foul garments on the table's corners and went in search of 4,000 calories. Food, spices, pots, and plates flew out of my dry bags, and, as the last of the sun left Winghaven, Mount Rainier glowed pink down Sound.

Ships can capture a sailor's heart, attracting like a lover and sustaining like a friend. Perhaps it is the sailor's reliance on this one vessel that creates such a bond, making the ship more than a workplace, more than a home—more like a partner in a marriage. There are those who are convinced that ships become living things. If you can believe that, you can begin to understand the mourning a sailor undergoes when a ship has outlived her usefulness, for ships usually die gracelessly.

On her final voyage, the USS Omaha *enters Rich Passage en route to Bremerton and the acetylene torch.*

The next day, as I entered Rich Passage—the entrance to Bremerton and the Puget Sound Naval Shipyard—the USS *Omaha*, an "attack submarine" of the Los Angeles class, passed me. She was in tow, decommissioned, headed to Bremerton to have her nuclear reactor removed. An expensive relic of the Cold War, she was one of the ships that mercifully never went to battle, but with her rounded bow and gray-black sail, she looked appropriately sinister for her Cold War

role. Now she was ending her life in quiet dignity in the backwater of the Puget Sound Naval Shipyard. And I needed to be a witness.

The tide shoved me toward Bremerton and the piers that held a history of ships. The carrier *Midway* was here, laid down in 1942. The USS *Missouri*, known as the "Mighty Mo," lay bow-out, towering over the smaller ships. On the quarterdeck of this 887-foot battleship, a commemorative seal marks the site of the Japanese surrender in World War II. But unnoticed in this armada were two small wooden minesweepers built in the spring and summer of 1955 by the Martinolich Shipyard. Now these last ships of the wooden navy, the USS *Enhance* and the USS *Esteem*, had returned home to an uncertain future.

As I passed down this long gray line, I photographed the ships using a long lens. In time, security people appeared on one dock and then another, binoculars aimed at me and radios active. I tucked the camera away to quell their excitement. With visions of my being strung from the yardarm, I turned for the southern side of the inlet, following the tide ebbing through Rich Passage.

By 6 P.M. I was between Bainbridge and Blake Islands, waiting for the Bremerton-bound Issaquah Class ferry *Chelan* to lumber by. I waved at the wheelhouse and the few topside passengers and then cut in behind them on course for the northeast point of Blake. This was a site I knew well, a Washington State Marine Park that encompasses the entire one-mile-square island. Located on the north side of a sand spit in the northwest corner of the island, the trail site is set against the forest amid a gaggle of beach logs and dune grass. It is not protected from the north wind, but from the site you can see Seattle eight miles distant, its downtown high-rises peeking over West Seattle's bulk. Tomorrow I'd be in Seattle. But for now I was staying at the finest natural piece of public property within sight of roughly 1.5 million people. The entire island is a forest returning; these trees gathering in the twilight would be considered old growth in about two hundred years. Mentally I willed them into maturity, knowing that I would not be around to see it happen. Two hundred years—I don't think my forearms would last that long.

Wise land use: camping within sight of Seattle, on Blake Island.

MARINE TRAIL CAMPSITE

HUMAN POWERED BEACHABLE

WATERCRAFT — CAMPING ONLY

Approaching the south point of Blake Island in a rare yellow sunset, paddlers make for camp.

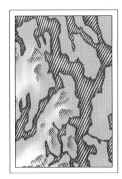

Carey Gersten—expectant father, computer-Internet marketer, and president of the Washington Water Trails Association—jumped at the chance to join me for the next leg of the Cascadia Marine Trail. We set schedules, negotiated the food, and met on the morning of June 20 at the south end of Seattle's Lake Union, where my Blake Island paddle had come to a halt five days before. Carey was relatively new to Seattle and

THE NEIGHBORHOOD SPIT

kayaking. Energetic, sharp-featured and clear-eyed, he reminded me of a hawk but with a degree in communications. As we crossed the heart of Lake Union, the downtown skyline visible over our left shoulders and the Fremont neighborhood dead ahead, we began to find a compatible paddling pace and conversational rhythm to last the week. Carey would stay with me as far as Bellingham, as we traveled north through the central Sound, paddling up Admiralty Inlet, ducking beneath Whidbey Island, and using Saratoga Passage to reach La Conner and Deception Pass. Today we would cross the Sound to Fay-Bainbridge State Park on the north end of Bainbridge Island, an easy ten miles.

It was Wednesday and Lake Union was alive with boats. Ahead of us, two small sloops were quietly escaping the city. One of them sounded an air horn for the Fremont Bridge, one long–one short blast; the bridge tender answered, counterweights rumbled, and the drawbridge opened high and wide. Carey and I smiled as we passed through, as

Point No Point
on the summer solstice.

if they had opened it just for us.

We were paddling the Lake Washington Ship Canal west toward its outlet on Puget Sound through Ballard, the waterfront community where I grew up. My grandmother's house had overlooked Ballard, the ship canal wending its way to the locks, the drawbridges rising, and toylike salmon boats chugging through. Along the shores the steel mill had belched orange-red steam, and from the ship repair yards had come the blue-white sparks of arc welders. In the center of the view, just beyond the Ballard Bridge, had towered the ricks of fresh-cut red-cedar boards and the massive smokestacks of the Seattle Cedar mill, the crowning landmark of Ballard's past.

Passing through the Hiram M. Chittenden Locks, Seattle.

As Carey and I paddled past the halibut schooners and the sites of long-gone cedar mills, we caught glimpses up into the street-grid of Ballard—the old brick streets, the rooftop of the Carnegie library, and the neighborhood where my grandfather's grocery still stands. For Carey it was a novel view of Ballard's maritime industry and uptown architecture. For me it was forty years of memories of the canal, the locks, and Puget Sound. As kids, my friends and I would bike to the bait docks on the edge of the Sound to fish and to deliver papers to the canal-side businesses. During college I lived on the waterway in graceful old derelict boats, and later I worked as a deckhand on tugs going through the locks and rowed the canal in a racing shell. Now it was as if the water's immutable presence had drawn me once again to fulfill the wish I'd had when I was ten, though not quite on the scale I'd imagined: to command a boat on the canal, sailing it between the drawbridges and well beyond the view from Grandmother's house.

At the Hiram M. Chittenden Locks, we encountered our one and only stoplight on the trip. Together with two sailboats and a few commercial craft, we waited at a holding pier before locking down to the Sound. Opened on July 4, 1917, by the U.S. Army Corps of Engineers (the $3.3 million project coming in $15,705 *under budget!*), the locks raised the tidal lagoon of Salmon Bay to 26 feet to link Puget Sound to Lake Union and Lake Washington. As the stoplight turned from red to green, we glided into the small lock, our bow and stern lines ready. The lockmaster directed us to go alongside two boats: a Thunderbird, the classic plywood 26-foot sloop of the 1950s, took Carey; I came alongside a powerboat named *Buffalo Soldier*. With an alarm-clock ring the fifty-foot-tall, fifteen-foot-wide riveted doors closed and we dropped, the water boiling about us. Not more than a minute later, the lock doors began to open; we let go of our mother ships and, waving to the sightseers (this is one of Seattle's greatest free tourist attractions), paddled into Puget Sound.

It was a warm and beautiful day as we pointed straight across the Sound toward Fay-Bainbridge. Falling in together about ten feet apart, the ideal talking distance for kayakers, Carey Gersten and I learned about each other. Carey was from upstate New York and of Jewish, Russian-Orthodox, and Irish-Catholic stock—an unusual lineage for a seafarer. His love of the outdoors brought him to Seattle in 1989, and a weekend at the annual West Coast Sea Kayak Symposium convinced him to both buy a kayak and join a small group espousing a trail system through the Sound. Carey reflected, "Kayaking was something I could do on my own: You can get in a boat and go out whenever and wherever you feel like it. It was the adventure in kayaking where there's no set paths that got me interested in the Cascadia Marine Trail. With increasing urbanization, I knew I was losing the ability to wander off. We had to come

The Fremont Bridge draws open for a sloop transiting the Lake Washington Ship Canal.

up with an organized freedom."

Carey not only joined the Washington Water Trails Association but became a board member and its most innovative booster. Now he was out riding the fenceline of his territory. Our first stop, the Fay-Bainbridge State Park trail site, is an open beach flanked by single-family homes. Like Vashon, forty-five-mile-square Bainbridge Island is a bedroom community of Seattle, and like Vashon it has become crowded. Carey called it the Yuppie Waterfront Kingdom, though neither one of us would forgo the chance to have our kayaks pulled up on our own Bainbridge beach.

That night we did have our kayaks on the beach edge, near the trail-site sign, which stood amid long-stranded beach logs. The following morning marked the solstice—June 21, the first day of summer—and I put on sunscreen as a rite of passage while the sun began to rise over a distant Ballard.

Three miles beyond Indianola, off Appletree Cove, we crossed the ferry lanes of that day's Kingston-Edmonds run. I eyed the ferry in the slip to make sure we wouldn't have to dodge her should she sail. She was the MV *Hyak*, a "super class" 160-car ferry built in 1967. One of thirty Washington State ferries on thirteen runs, she is a sturdy, utilitarian ship in one of the largest ferry fleets in the world. But as practical and efficient as today's ferry system is (a subject of continual debate at any ferry dock on a Sunday afternoon), it couldn't begin to match the romance and energy of the steamboat era on Puget Sound.

Poring over the well-respected *Marine History of the Pacific Northwest*, I counted 255 steamers registered in the Puget Sound district—mostly passenger and freight boats. That was in 1892, before the Alaska-Yukon gold rush made Seattle a boomtown and before the greatest waves of immigrants settled in. Because of their sheer numbers these side-wheelers, paddle wheelers, and propeller-driven, wood-burning, coal-burning, and oil-fueled craft were called the "mosquito fleet," and they made up one of the finest mass transit systems the world has ever seen. There were so many vessels that rate wars lasted for years on some runs, with low fares creating boomtowns like Burton and Quartermaster Harbor

As morning light bathes Bainbridge Island and the Olympic peaks, a ferry approaches Winslow.

Readying the kayaks for an easy day's paddle from Fay-Bainbridge State Park to Point No Point.

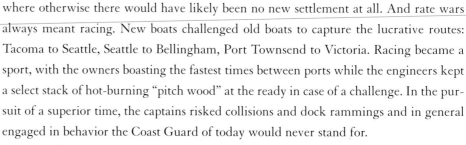

where otherwise there would have likely been no new settlement at all. And rate wars always meant racing. New boats challenged old boats to capture the lucrative routes: Tacoma to Seattle, Seattle to Bellingham, Port Townsend to Victoria. Racing became a sport, with the owners boasting the fastest times between ports while the engineers kept a select stack of hot-burning "pitch wood" at the ready in case of a challenge. In the pursuit of a superior time, the captains risked collisions and dock rammings and in general engaged in behavior the Coast Guard of today would never stand for.

But the newspapers loved it, and the people loved it. Which boat you favored or rode became so personal that it divided towns. In Poulsbo those who traveled on the original *Hyak* refused to talk to or do business with their rivals on the *Verona*—for seven years. Boats became as loved as baseball teams. The *Flyer* carried millions of passengers without a mishap while setting world records for reliability and mileage. The 221-foot *Tacoma* was billed in 1914 as the "fastest single-screw [propeller] ship in the world." She dominated the Seattle–Tacoma run at twenty knots for sixteen years. The *Virginia V* ran between Seattle and Tacoma, making stops along the way; in particular, she carried Camp Fire Girls to Camp Sealth on Vashon Island. She had enough contract business to enable her to outlast all the hundreds of steamboats before her. The last of the original mosquito fleet, today she is undergoing refit so she can sail again.

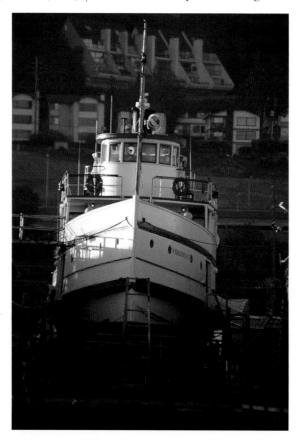

The Virginia V*, the last of the steamboats on Puget Sound, gets a refit at Lake Union Dry Dock.*

By noon Carey and I were above Apple Cove Point, keeping to the beach. The sun's glare was unremitting, and the pace of paddling and conversation we'd set the day before slowed with the tide. Stripped down to my spray skirt, with sweat steaming my sunglasses, I would stop paddling at times and drift, trailing my hands in the cool of the Sound. One hundred feet out from the shore, the bottom looked to be fifteen feet beneath my keel, and I watched for crabs and small congregations of perch to

Sun rays over the Puget Sound basin, Point No Point.

ward off the monotony. I spread more sunscreen across my forearms and paddled into the afternoon. By 3 P.M. we had finally finished our run and stood off Point No Point, a proposed trail site: a spit with a Coast Guard lighthouse and what appeared to be the entire population of the north Kitsap Peninsula.

THE PORT MADISON RUN

When marine designer Jack Kutz was twelve years old, he rode both the Hyak *and the* Vashon *steamer ferries between Seattle and Port Madison. Now seventy-five, Jack remembers the mosquito fleet like it was yesterday: "There's nothing like riding on a steamboat. It sticks with you all your life. They leaned and rolled just from the force of the wind! The more dignified folks sat in the main salon on the upper deck in wicker chairs. The working folks usually sat on the lower deck as a matter of preference. A mahogany bench ran from the bow to the stern on each side, with the steam engine exposed in the center. The closer you got to the engine room uptakes [the casing around the steampipes], the warmer it got. Aft, there was a low railing, and when [the steamer] backed down, you'd get sprayed. You could hear every command, every bell, the rudder thumping . . . you could see the . . . big propellers. They went fast—12 to 14 knots—though you felt like they were going faster. There is nothing like them today. Nothing."*

We landed on the beach between bathing-suited teenagers and a pack of kids building a driftwood fort. Fishermen stood on the point casting for king salmon, and seasoned lovers walked into the wind hand in hand. Carey and I stretched and walked out the kinks, joining the citizens of what we came to call the Principality of Point No Point.

Charles Wilkes named it "No Point" for its un-geography. Unlike Point Robinson on Vashon or Alki off West Seattle, points that jut prominently into the Sound, Point No Point is a bump, an easy forty-degree turn for any ship on the standard inbound or outbound course. But what a bump! Beyond the multitude of salmon fishermen and tide rips is a sweeping view south across open water to the high-rises of Seattle over twenty miles away, as well as a view north along the Cascade Range to lofty Mount Baker rising 10,778 feet above sea level. To the west is twenty-mile-long Admiralty Inlet, the entrance to the Strait of Juan de Fuca and a hint of open sea.

A sudden shout stopped us in our tracks. A large man by the name of Lance had saved our kayaks from floating adrift in the breaking waves. Suitably embarrassed, we dragged them up above the previous tideline and thanked him. We unloaded, making short trips up the beach to place our gear in the shade of the beach logs. Carey had cooking duty for the evening, leaving me to watch the cast of Fellini-esque characters stream by.

Families were announced by a dog, which was quickly followed by one kid and then another. They swept by, splashing and laughing; the parents stopped to look wistfully at the kayaks, then hurried on as their pride-and-joys disappeared around the point. The solo beach scavengers approached more slowly, heads down, inching along like the periwinkles they were collecting. One enterprising local struggled with a monumental piece of driftwood, its weight driving his wheelbarrow into the sand. A woman thundered past atop a fine Appaloosa, turning and wheeling in the shallows, spray flying, her body light on the horse's back.

Then came a short woman in a blue-and-white sundress walking two low-to-the-beach Scottish terriers. I cannot resist Scotties. As they played tug-of-war with a stick and I tried (unsuccessfully) to photograph them, the woman told us of last week's big event. Pointing toward the base of the spit where the second growth rose up the hill, she said there were two bald eagles in the firs: "You have to watch out for them; they tried to make off with a dachshund last week. It needed over a hundred stitches." Carey tried

Carey Gersten's turn to cook dinner. Hot spice extra.

not to laugh as the wet, black Scotties romped along the beach and their mistress warily eyed the forest.

We were surrounded by people who were shyly advancing toward, flirting with, or immersing themselves in the Sound. They had come to Point No Point to be on the edge, to find fun, joy, solace with this living body of water. They took salmon, shells, even driftwood in order to touch something strong and natural. I do not know if they loved this beach in particular, if they felt the pull of their aqueous natures, or if it was simply an off day in pro sports. Perhaps it was the fact that it was the first day of

summer and, coincidentally, the hottest day in June. Still, I couldn't help feeling that their presence here embodied our attachment to the Sound.

We settled back that evening with dinner in our laps and an eye on the trees in case the eagles were considering larger game. At some point Carey wondered about the tide, steadily rising toward our camp. I checked the tidebook and my watch, eyed the tents, and took another bite. Midway through our dinner the wake of a passing container ship curled ashore, the swash rushing up the beach to die at our feet. We settled back and finished dinner as the twilight went on and on . . . then moved the tents.

One day after the start of summer we woke at 5 A.M. to a raw, cold darkness. The wind was from the south gusting to fifteen knots, the Sound lidded by a rough set of clouds. How the weather could change so quickly mystified us. It was as if yesterday had been a dream, Point No Point a Camelot, and now it was time to meet the reality of a fast-moving low front. We had an ambitious distance to paddle as we launched into the day: twenty-one miles to Camano State Park. I did not launch dry, which caused my mood to match the conditions.

We paddled across the Sound toward the southern end of Whidbey Island, crossing the shipping lanes in the trough of the wave train that had been building all the way from Vashon. Together we set a common landmark to paddle toward and kept within shouting distance as the wind and waves steadily increased. In water like this, when the distance between wave crests is not much greater than the length of one's boat, a kayaker can get into trouble. After a few breaking whitecaps slapped first me and then Carey, we began to moan to the weather gods. Approaching Whidbey, we paddled atop a shallow shelf, once a bluff but now a wave-cut bench sticking out a

Pier pilings coated with sea life, Langley, Whidbey Island.

Admiralty Inlet from the bluffs of Ebey's Landing, Whidbey Island.

mile from Scatchet Head. It was rougher here, as the water from Possession Sound ebbed around Whidbey and flowed up and over the bench to meet the waves and wind from the south. The waves ganged up on each other, forcing us to paddle from crest to sudden crest. We stuttered our strokes to meet the random wave patterns and kept our balance by always finding solid water. As experienced paddlers, we faced no real danger, but we took this as a warning of what the Sound could do when the wrong forces mixed. Noting calmer seas closer in toward Possession Point, we damp little seafarers turned and surfed toward Whidbey and out of the chaos.

Volunteers plant the first trail-site sign, at Camano Island State Park.

The rest of the morning we had the wind at our backs and, though we fought a strong current, we paddled in a more sheltered part of Puget Sound called Possession Sound, named by Captain Vancouver to commemorate the spot where he took possession of "New Albion" for "His Britannic Majesty, his heirs and successors" on June 4, 1792. This is the "back-door" route that the old tugboat skippers took with their fragile log tows, avoiding the rougher waters on the west side of Whidbey Island. Keeping to the island side of Possession Sound and passing Everett in the hazy distance, we paddled into the sunshine.

By 1 P.M. we had entered the waters of Saratoga Passage, which separates Whidbey and Camano Islands. There was no more sign of the low front as we paddled into the gentrified town of Langley, found a busy restaurant, and sat down, a damp and somewhat scruffy-looking advance patrol from the Principality of Point No Point. By the time we were back in the boats, we had brownies and baseball scores (Seattle beat Chicago) and no wind whatsoever. But an hour later, four miles short of Camano State Park, our destination of the day, we paddled into a steady, stubborn, twenty-knot headwind. I wondered if we should expect snow by nightfall.

It took us hours to make landfall. We arrived exhausted at 6 P.M. on a rocky, barnacled beach. Our trail site was well away from the other campers, tucked along a path just up from the beach. It was not the best site so far, nor was it the worst; but it had the distinction of being the first site dedicated on the Cascadia Marine Trail—the site where the first work party of board members and volunteers hacked away at the vegetation, and where the core group of trail advocates erected the first of many MARINE TRAIL CAMPSITE signs and stood back in pride. Carey and I uncorked a bottle of wine and toasted the many hands that wouldn't let this idea die. Then we ate a large pasta dinner and slept the sleep of the dead.

A cool sun over Camano Island.

Four miles north of Camano Island, Carey and I paddled off the edge of the chart called "Puget Sound." In twelve days I had paddled 214 miles across this creased and worn map. As I folded it into its final square and squeezed it into the chart case beneath the stiff, untried chart called "Strait of Juan de Fuca to Strait of Georgia," I was at the halfway point of my journey, approaching a new and different marine world.

THE CURVE OF THE EARTH

Instead of the narrow corridors and passes of the South Sound and Admiralty Inlet, the waters ahead were a convergence of sounds and straits swept by stronger currents and a faster-paced energy. Here we would find a climate warm enough to grow cactus, and waters alive with orcas, pelagic bird colonies, and the taste of the open ocean.

The Cascadia Marine Trail was at its best here, with a high concentration of sites spread throughout the area. Our destination was Deception Pass State Park, seventeen and a half miles distant. According to the current tables, if we were more than twenty minutes late to the pass, we'd have to buck half the Pacific surging back through its narrow channels. Deep in the heart of Saratoga Passage, the calmest and most featureless backwater of the northern Sound, I paddled with an almost childlike sense of adventure. Carey figured it was the coffee, but I knew it was more the challenge of making the pass, treading our way through new country. Our world was scaled down to a pair of seventeen-foot boats in

Late summer on Isohis Slough, the
Skagit River estuary in north Puget Sound.

The rattling call and buzz of a long-billed marsh wren (Telmatodytes palustris) *is an unmistakable declaration of territory.*

which three-foot waves were just even with the top of our heads. Once-familiar shores were landfalls to be won. The weather became a serious guessing game. Food became fuel. A Therm-a-Rest seat and a warm cup of coffee represented luxury. There was no pressure, no doubts, just a pass to make and a site to claim.

By 1 P.M., as we paddled off the mouth of the Skagit River estuary, it was clear we'd make Deception Pass at low-water slack. Carey and I relaxed our pace to enjoy the dramatically different landscape ahead. The sand, silt, and cobble layer-cake geology of the South Sound had given way to something more substantial. For the first time we encountered islands with rocky shores and cliff faces of sedimentary and volcanic rock. Ika, Goat, Hope, and Skagit Islands rose like forested gumdrops amid the mudflats and channels, the broccoli and tulip fields. It was an idyllic place of snow geese, Dutch barns, and towns nestled in a topography that delighted the eye and hid the pass that appeared ahead with a suddenness that startled us.

Captain Vancouver named it Deception Pass because of this hidden quality. He shied away from entering it with his ships, choosing to work them south to round Whidbey Island rather than risk their wooden hulls in the current and whirlpools. As we passed forested Hoypus Point, the shore began rising to cliffs as the current steadily increased. Quickly we were forced to decide which channel to take—the big two-hundred-yard-wide main pass or the tiny fifty-yard-wide northern passage known as Canoe Pass. As we were in human-powered watercraft, Canoe Pass had our name written all over it. Since the main current was forcing us left, we paddled right, and right some more. Then we were into it.

We could hear rapids downstream where the channel curved around the buttress of Pass Island. I let myself be drawn into a calm, deep-green, V-shaped ramp of water that ended in noisy confusion where the outgoing tide fell into the center of the narrowing

"Distributaries" is the term naturalists use to describe the branching of the Skagit River estuary.

canyon. My bow pierced a set of standing rapids about two feet high, the white water buffeting me. The boils and cross-currents of the outwash wrenched our kayaks first one way and then the other. But in a few moments we were into calmer currents, and the headlands of the pass dropped away. A few strokes more and we relaxed the grip on our paddle shafts. Before us lay the Strait of Juan de Fuca; beneath us was the unmistakable rise and fall of the distant Pacific.

Bowman Bay lies on the north side of Deception Pass, facing the strait. Protected by an arm of cliffs and sea stacks topped by meadows and conifers, it is a quiet enclave compared to the jostle of the pass. Yet there are people everywhere: climbing on rocks and cliffs, hiking the forest trails, fishing from outboards. We paddled in and landed, joining a population unlike the one at Point No Point. Folks here behaved like new visitors to the water's edge: tentative, clumsy, exuberant— even violent, if you included the kid busy hacking away at the wild roses with a three-foot piece of driftwood. This was Deception Pass State Park, created in 1921 and now grown to over 3,500 acres. It is the most popular and, to my taste, the most beautiful park in the state of Washington.

In need of restrooms, a shower, and 4,000 calories, Carey and I landed in a mass of rotting seaweed and slimed ashore. It began to rain. That was fine with us. There was no designated marine trail-site sign, but a ranger confirmed the location and we camped above the beach beneath tall, well-spaced firs. (The park has since moved the site away from the other campers to the south end of the bay.) As we ate in a dark picnic shelter near our beached kayaks, we watched a father tell his young son about kayaks and what we were doing. To our surprise, he knew about the Cascadia Marine Trail, which he described as the "kayak highway." Carey and I smiled; we had never heard that phrase before. It struck us as being both a utilitarian and an evocative description.

Boom logs in a low-tide dusk, the south fork of the Skagit River estuary in north Puget Sound.

The unnerving sound of unseen rapids marks Canoe Pass, the northern approach to Deception Pass.

Old-growth timber cloaks a glacial-rounded island south of La Conner.

A relict is a "persistent remnant of an otherwise extinct flora," a "relief feature remaining after other parts have disappeared." The next morning we backtracked through Deception Pass and, in rounding Hoypus Point, I realized we were paddling past a relict forest, an ancient grove of old growth that extended right down to the tideline. Nowhere in the two-hundred-odd miles I'd traveled so far had I seen trees over four hundred years old rising up 170 feet to eagle's nests. The Hoypus Point forest and, as it turns out, the trees of Hope Island across the channel are some of the last stands of the magnificent forest that once rimmed the entire 2,000-mile coastline of the Sound. Laying my paddle down, I drifted toward a false point overhung with ancient hemlock and spruce, their branches framing the pristine Hope Island. I felt protective toward this lonely grove, truly a refugium amid the bustle of mechanized humanity. Fortunately, Hoypus is one of nine forest patches within the state park system that are designated as Natural Forest Areas, with their own restrictions and guidelines for public use. In this particular little-known forest, public use consists of the faint paths left by red-legged frogs, black-tailed deer, and Douglas squirrels.

Taking liberties with our three-inch draft, from Hoypus Carey and I made a bee-line for the south entrance of Swinomish Channel, skimming over the flats between Hope and Goat Islands. We were intent on an easy day: brunch in the town of La Conner and a camp on Saddlebag Island.

La Conner is as beautiful a picture as the Northwest can paint. Approaching from the south, squeezing in between McGlinn and Fidalgo Islands, we came upon it suddenly: a line of river warehouses, floats and pilings, gillnetters, and one fine schooner, with church steeples and Victorian windows beyond. (On a better day Mount Baker, 43 miles distant, commands the upper left-hand corner of this postcard of a town.)

Although the National Register of Historic Places preserves its 1880s façade, La Conner's mercantile energy in the 1990s bursts through every historic seam. We secured our kayaks on the inside of a pier, grabbed our water containers, and clomped up the gangplank to scare the tourists. We scouted for breakfast and found a line waiting at a restaurant with good food but decor so excruciatingly cute I doubted they'd seen a pair of red ball boots tracking in mud since the day they first opened for business. They let us in anyway.

Carey and I departed La Conner with the Mariners on a winning streak (seven out of ten games) and a massive cumulonimbus system building over the surrounding tulip fields. Staying to the left bank of the Swinomish Channel—what had once been the bed of the Skagit River—we dodged powerboats and rain showers to reach Padilla Bay and Saddlebag Island. A Department of Natural Resources park and Cascadia Marine Trail site, the island is truly shaped like saddlebags—the "bags" being rock bluffs topped by meadow and forest, with a fine harbor in between them.

We came ashore, unloaded, and found the trail site roughly seventy feet into a dense second-growth forest, where we discovered that the metal trail sign had been hacked almost in two. The vandal who did this spent an inordinate amount of time with the wrong tool for the job—a rock, as near as we could figure. But before we could take the vandalism too seriously, we encountered a human-powered watercraft and saw the first people I'd

Across the channel from La Conner lies the Swinomish Indian reservation.

met actually using the Trail. Out of the sunset from Guemes Channel came a double kayak. Carey found his binoculars and we critiqued their approach: two guys, young, paddles out of synch, new to kayaking and new to the area, judging from the way they checked and rechecked a map too small to be a chart. We met them at the beach and invited them to join us once they'd settled in.

Brant and Chad lived in New York, where somehow they had heard about the Cascadia Marine Trail. They flew to Seattle, rented a kayak and, with rudimentary map, tidebook, and state park annual passes in hand, set out for a five-day adventure. No real preparation, no water safety training, just a desire to do it.

Carey and I were both charmed and appalled. The discovery that "our first" users had no real sea kayaking experience raised questions about what role we, as developers of the Trail, needed to play to ensure the safety of these brand-new paddlers. "Disclaimer" seemed to be the word of the day. And then we turned to the job of educating our new companions. Clearly they were dazzled by the natural beauty of the route, despite the view of the lights from the Texaco and Shell refineries burning like a city two miles across Padilla Bay.

We suggested they paddle with us the following day as we headed north over a flat-calm, blue-hued sea. For Chad and Brant it amounted to a verbal crash course on currents, for we were on the edge of the San Juan Islands, an area known by local paddlers for its powerful, sometimes deadly tide races. To safely paddle these waters, kayakers need to be familiar with a remarkable navigation tool titled *Current Atlas/Atlas des Courants, Juan de Fuca Strait to/á Strait of Georgia* and known colloquially as the *Current Atlas*. For over a decade two scientists, W. S. Huggett of the Canadian Hydrographic Service and P. B. Crean of

Brant and Chad approach Saddlebag Island, with Dot Island and Padilla Bay to their right.

the Ocean Physics Division, Environment Canada, have compiled statistics on tides and currents in this area and displayed them on a series of maps with the currents represented by patterns of arrows. With this book and a copy of "Washburn's Tables," first-time visitors can plan their routes with a reasonable assurance of what they will encounter.

During our paddle toward Lummi Island, our New York novices showed clear signs of competence and common sense. We mapped out the currents for their intended route and talked about the anomalies of the San Juans—morning fog, ship traffic, fast-moving small boats, changing weather patterns, and raccoons in the night—before we parted at the south end of Lummi. They were bound for Cypress Island and on into the San Juans, which boast the richest field of sites on the Cascadia Marine Trail. I was steeling myself for the longest crossing of the trip, from Lummi Island across the southern Georgia Strait to the loneliest site on the Trail—Point Roberts. Carey would not be accompanying me; he had a board meeting to attend. After covering eighty-two miles with me along the main trunk of the system, he could return to the Washington Water Trails board with salt water in his veins and a much clearer appreciation of what else needed to be done to the "kayak highway." At noon we parted company, Carey heading toward Bellingham and home, I to camp at the Department of Natural Resources trail site on Lummi Island.

THE NUTRIENT TRAP

At the head of Skagit Bay is the estuary and salt marsh of the Skagit River. From a distance, it is a line of cattails and cottonwoods—but hidden in the marshgrass and willow is a maze of sloughs carrying the flow of the Skagit's north and south forks down from the Cascade Range. Each year the delta "progrades," or advances a little more into the bay, slowly filling the basin with silt from the fall floods and spring runoff. When the river reaches flood stage, the water is fast and thick with glacial milk, forest duff, even whole trees. Once the flood enters the sloughs, the snags catch and tangle in the estuary channels, but the silt runs free with the current until it too falls out of the main flow in heavy deposits atop the estuarine islands. When the floods recede and the tide returns, the depressions formed by the deposited silt become nutrient traps that collect the detritus of the land and sea in layer after layer of stored food. This is what makes a salt marsh the richest marine environment in the Sound.

From a secluded cove on the lee of high-ridged Lummi Island, I mentally mapped the distance, pictured the currents, and weighed the risks of my solo paddle to Point Roberts. The southern Georgia Strait is twice as big a body of water as any basin in Puget Sound. Bounded by the San Juan and Canadian Gulf Islands to the southwest and the

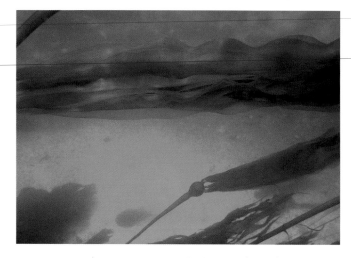

Bull kelp (Nereocystis luetkeana) *signals the rise of a reef and a high concentration of sea life.*

Washington and British Columbia mainland to the north, its width varies from six to ten miles and its length is roughly twenty-five miles. My course would take me right down the middle of it for twenty-two miles of continuous paddling. True, it was not Dover-to-Calais, but without favorable winds and fair tides I would have to stop short.

After a breakfast of hot Ralston and Cream of Wheat, my grandmother's stalwart blend from Ballard mornings, I gave added scrutiny to my day kit, knowing that once under way there'd be no retrieving anything that wasn't ready at hand. Extra water bottles were stashed beside my seat. A lunch of two peanut butter and jelly bagels, two apples, and one orange made the daybag. I checked the radio for battery power and confirmed the presence of flares, towline, paddle float, and compass. Lastly, I looked again at the *Current Atlas*, which showed an incoming tide moving at one to one and a half knots straight to Point Roberts.

To catch the current I paddled a mile west of the north end of Lummi, just entering the Vessel Traffic Lane that leads out from Rosario Strait. There were no tankers abroad, no container ships in sight, just a salmon seiner hull down, making its way north. As I turned toward Canada I looked for Point Roberts, a peninsula with a distinctive high bluff jutting south from the British Columbia mainland. I couldn't see it. I checked the chart and made a compass bearing. I still couldn't see it, though both the rise of Vancouver Island and the foothills of the Coast Range were visible. I was looking at the curve of the earth. I secured my compass to the deck and aligned my direction with where Point Roberts ought to be, all the while experiencing the eerie feeling of paddling on a compass course toward an invisible landfall.

"Plash" is the sound and the word for striking water. At sixty to seventy paddle plashes per minute, I'd create 31,200 strokes to reach Point Roberts. I reminded myself not to count them. Five miles distant from Lummi, I passed buoy BR "B" 1Qk Fl "gong" as marked on my chart to indicate an "isolated danger." Buoy B marked the mass of Alden Bank, a submerged ridge extending northwest from Lummi Island, rising from a six-hundred-foot depth to a mesalike peak just seventeen feet below the surface. On the chart I could read the symbols: small branches signaled extensive kelp beds anchored to a rocky (*Rky*) summit coated in gravel (*G*), with mud (*M*) and shells (*Sh*) covering the gentler eastern slopes. I noted my time and made a compass course across the little seamount.

Eastward facing, well forested, and secluded—the Lummi Island trail site.

A cormorant fishing for herring, sand lances, or sculpins circled my kayak as I passed over the rising bank. All around me I noticed feed welling up. The not-so-tiny zooplankters were the shrimplike copepods, I could guess, but there may have been clouds of euphausiids (krill) or the tiny, lance-shaped little barracudas known as chaetognaths, all brought to the surface by the billions in a spiral of food-chain feeding. For three miles I paddled a gently confused sea amid wheeling seabirds and shadowing seals. I passed a few salmon fishermen trolling in the near distance and a couple of anchored boats with dive flags flying. No one seemed to pay me the slightest attention.

About an hour and four miles later, I reached Buoy A and rechecked my watch to calculate my speed between buoys while taking bites of lunch: sixty minutes times four miles divided by my actual time of seventy minutes equals 3.4 miles per hour. With twelve miles still to go, I had three hours to paddle. I took another bite and a gulp of water, anxious to resume my passage. I stared at 300° magnetic on the compass course, then looked up, and there was Point Roberts, a smudge of land on a faintly rounded horizon. That would be dinner. This was lunch. But conditions were changing; I would have to eat on the road. Refitting my spray skirt, I took a huge bite out of the last bagel and brought Boato back up to speed.

A CUBIC METER OF PUGET SOUND

I asked Richard Strickland, an oceanographer at the University of Washington, what might be found in one cubic meter of seawater suspended over Puget Sound's Alden Bank.

"Dissolved gases and minerals—phosphorus, carbon, potassium, cobalt, zinc, and salt, to name a few—and with tidal upwelling, the waters of the bank would be rich in nitrogen. Nitrogen is the fertilizer that feeds the phytoplankton . . . a community of one-celled green-brown algae [that includes] diatoms, no bigger than a pencil point, [which] are most likely the greatest in number over Alden Bank. They like wave action, something that stirs up the water. Predators to the phytoplankton, and each other, are the zooplankton. They range from one-celled protozoans to a multitude of multicellular animals. Along with copepods, euphausiids, and chaetognaths, are the shrimp-like mysids and amphipods, larval forms of crabs, segmented worms, mussels, and other creatures—all within this one cubic meter of saltwater."

If you removed all the water from our cubic meter, what would be the biomass that remained? After some calculations, Strickland answered, "No bigger than a pea."

The southwest wind that had been a congenial friend throughout the morning was now getting a little pushy. Waves averaging two to three feet high were running faster than I was. I listened for the bigger ones, the waves that would break on top of me, swirling water around my waist and throwing the kayak off course; they came in trains of six to eight, their noisy, tumbling advance signaling their arrival. One by one they lifted Boato's stern, surging me forward until the bow got buried in the wave ahead and I slowed radically. Only with a burst of sprint-paddling could I stay with these bigger waves, surfing their slopes. My 3.4 knots rose to seven as Boato tobogganed along.

Once I was surfing I could stop paddling and use my blade as a rudder, my body adding English as I leaned to one side or the other to keep the bow pointed toward Point Roberts. I ran with a wave until it lost its energy—in this sea maybe forty yards, sometimes a hundred. Then I hustled to catch a bigger one. I covered acres of ocean in that manner, spray flying, water creeping in, lungs working at capacity. Eventually I got tired, reined in my exuberance, and resumed a steady cruising pace toward what was now a much closer Point Roberts. My arrival was a private celebration.

The salt marsh of the Skagit, looking toward La Conner hills.

Bound for the San Juan Islands, I left Point Roberts at 4:48 the next morning, a tiny ship beneath a gray-blue tent of cloud. The wind was head-on at a steady five to eight knots that sent spray back across my face in cold slaps. Though my twelve-mile voyage to Patos Island paralleled the southern Gulf Islands—Galiano, Main, and Saturna, two to three miles distant—I might as well have been in the middle of the Pacific.

ANYWHERE I LIKE

By 7 A.M. I was just off the three-mile-wide entrance to Boundary Pass (the channel that connects Georgia Strait with Haro Strait and the Strait of Juan de Fuca) when I discovered I was not alone on the high seas. An outbound log carrier passed me a mile and a half to starboard. As she turned to enter the pass, another big ship, a beamy grain carrier inbound for Vancouver, came into view. I checked the chart to make sure I was well outside the shipping lanes. I was, but so was the grain carrier. Not more than a mile away, I watched as her bow came around in my direction. If the pilot checked her swing too soon, I'd better be on the radio to her pilot. In the meantime I changed course. Looking down at my dry-cased marine radio, I rehearsed the procedures to raise them on channel 16, the "distress, safety, and calling" channel. I would say, "To the motor vessel inbound east end of Boundary Pass, there is a seventeen-foot kayak approximately one mile off your starboard bow. I will pass starboard to starboard. . . ."

The height of Yellow Island's wildflower bloom: Indian
paintbrush, purple camas, and western buttercup.

Fortunately, the carrier continued her turn and missed me by a good half mile, the crew on the bridge most likely unaware of my early-morning progress.

Mapping the route through the San Juans, from Active Cove on Patos Island.

On a map, the San Juan Islands appear to form a star cluster. Like the Pleiades in the night sky, these 172 named islands are their own cosmos, a ring of outer islands protecting a core of smaller ones insulated by the combined waters of Puget Sound, Georgia Strait, and the Strait of Juan de Fuca. This archipelago is flanked by mountains—the Olympics to the south, the Cascades to the east, and the ridge of Vancouver Island to the north—each boldly blocking and shaping the weather, bringing a warm, dry climate to the islands, creating a Mediterranean experience in an evergreen landscape.

These islands, islets, reefs, and rocks are not undiscovered. In the summer powerboats, sailboats, small cruise ships, whale-watching tours, and sea kayakers fill the channels and passes, creating navigational mayhem. The larger islands—San Juan, Orcas, Lopez, and Shaw—are serviced by Washington State ferries from the mainland town of Anacortes, ferries that are so overwhelmed in high season that four-hour waits for a two-hour voyage are not unusual. The bucolic, lightly forested archipelago has suffered a 300 percent population increase over the past twenty years, while the number of tourists drawn to the islands each year is approaching one million. Despite the onslaught, it is still a rural-to-wild island paradise with a slow-paced lifestyle that remains the envy and dream of almost every island visitor.

On the outer edge of those dreams is 1.3-mile-long Patos Island, the northernmost island of the San Juans and my destination for this morning. Owned by the Bureau of

Land Management, it is still wild; no 5,500-square-foot retirement villas are planned for Alden Point, just a Coast Guard automated lighthouse. Nor is there a single real-estate sign in Active Cove—just a campsite, an outhouse, and two picnic tables above the natural harbor. Patos, like its eastward neighbors Sucia and Matia, looks much like the coastal islands of Maine: an all-rock foundation flattened and elongated by the glaciers, with a dense fir forest on top. (All three islands were named by the Spanish in 1792; Patos means "duck," Sucia "foul" (for its reefs), and Matia "no protection.")

Paddling these island waters are nearly 30 sea kayak guide companies, local kayak clubs, and independent paddlers—as well as those traveling the Cascadia Marine Trail—making the San Juan Islands the most popular sea kayak destination in the world.

Fortunately, land in the San Juans has long had a high priority among state parks and Department of Natural Resources acquisition efforts. The Washington Water Trails Association's alliance with these agencies quickly created the richest collection of sites on the Trail—at last count there were sixteen, five within a day's paddle of Patos Island. Here there are no marathon paddles, and with many different sites to choose from, canoeists, rowers, or paddlers like Chad and Brant can stop short if the weather changes, go with the tides or winds, or avoid a crowded site in favor of one that's less populated.

At Patos I had options of my own to consider. Some paddling friends planned to join me two days hence at a site called Spencer Spit on Lopez Island. At the pace I'd been maintaining, I could go almost anywhere in the five-hundred-square-mile archipelago and still make the rendezvous. To the west was Stuart Island, tempting for its beautiful bays and harbors. Going east I could follow the wild, high shore of Orcas to

TRADITIONAL KAYAKS

Randy Monge builds kayaks on Orcas Island, using skills he learned from a series of workshops with Alaska Aleut elders and from Bellingham's George Dyson, one of the first contemporary builders of centuries-old kayak designs. Randy's boats feature a wooden frame and a bright-white Hypalon-fabric skin, and were copied from the Aleut kayak, called Ikyan, or what Russian fur traders once called Baidarkas. Each has a unique notched or bifurcated bow, so that the lower jut of the hull acts as a cutwater to drive the kayak through the seas, while the upper half acts as a lift. Randy thinks this curious design is particularly useful in surf landings, allowing the Ikyan to stay on the surface when a conventionally bowed kayak would dive. And though slightly beamier than their ancestors, these new lightweight craft still retain the V hull and wood-frame flexibility that made them fast, efficient kayaks in all sorts of weather. The only concession to the modern day is that the cockpits have been enlarged from a tight-fitting oval to more of a keyhole shape to accommodate the somewhat larger paddlers of today.

visit the atoll-like Clark and Barnes Islands, and then turn toward the center of the San Juans through Peavine Pass. But I chose President Channel between Waldron and Orcas, the direct course to the very heart of the San Juans.

To reach President Channel I had to cross a five-mile stretch of open water that hid both West Bank, part of the Sucia Island foundation, and Parker Reef, an extension of Orcas Island's north shore. From Patos the crossing looks innocent enough, but when the tides and currents overriding these submerged hills meet with a change in the weather, a mean sea works against a small boat. Unfortunately, the current maps are not detailed enough to warn the unsuspecting paddler of danger, and the charts, drawn for bigger vessels, fail to mark the area for tide rips. I read the chart's marine topography and imagined the tidal flows before setting out, then set a course to stay clear of the confusion.

As I approached the West Bank, I could both hear the white-sound of waves breaking without rhythm or rhyme and see the ragged line of pinnacle waves notching the immediate horizon. I paddled to stay west of it, comfortable in the disturbed waters, skirting the edge of the maelstrom, its flotsam swirling in a shivering, multi-wavelet dance. By the time I was clear, I was a half-mile west of my intended course.

With the wind rising from the southwest, I stayed close to the west beach of Orcas, where I found myself sharing the road with some Dall's porpoise on one side and a marten or mink slinking along the other. The high cliffs of Turtleback Mountain stretched up and away to my left. There were eagles in the relict firs to watch, and boulders in the shallows to avoid. Abreast of Orcas Knob, a sea mammal surfaced just off my bow. Sensing my presence, it turned to look at me, and for a moment we studied each other. I had never seen anything like it. It was not a doe-eyed harbor seal face, nor did it have the golden retriever face of the Steller's sea lion or the Frankenstein forehead of the California sea lion. No, this sea mammal was like a bad sculpture, a memento from God's high school

A Washington State ferry glides through the early evening stillness near Spencer Spit.

Waldron Island and President Channel, the San Juans.

shop. It had a massive head, a face of jowls and folds, and a proboscis of considerable size.

It turns out that I had crossed courses with a rare migrating two-ton male northern elephant seal, also known as *Mirounga angustirostris*. He dove and I decided to wait, hoping he'd surface nearby. I waited. I paddled upwind, staying closer to shore to give him open water. I waited some more. I waited, not realizing that my elephant seal would be at least twenty minutes beneath the surface, deep-diving after dogfish. I checked the chart and found that I was suspended over a submarine wall that drops a sheer 600 feet (107 fathoms) no more than an eighth of a mile offshore.

Eventually the persistent wind forced me to continue my slog up this windy passage, paddling like hell at the points and easing up in the coves. Eleven and a half miles from Patos, I looked in on Jones Island, a state marine park and a trail site, paddling past the great-sunset camp that is perhaps the most coveted kayaker's spot in the islands. A mile farther I skirted eleven-acre Yellow Island with its lover's cabin on its western point, one of nine small islands known as the Wasp Islands, an insect-size archipelgo along the northern margin of San Juan Channel.

A chocolate lily (Fritillaria lanceolata) *opens to a Yellow Island sunrise.*

As perfect an island as I could imagine, Yellow Island saw its ownership pass in the spring of 1980 from the Dodd family to the Washington State chapter of the Nature Conservancy. This organization specializes in identifying and preserving rare and endangered plants, animals, and habitats such as Yellow Island, which has almost all the plants native to the San Juans.

The week before Yellow Island became a Conservancy preserve, I photographed the spring wildflower bloom (over 150 species) for the organization while Joe and Sally (Dodd) Hall prepared to leave the island to nature. I stayed in what I called the lover's cabin, part of Lew Dodd's (Sally's father) craftsman legacy—a small cottage hand-built of island rock and drift timbers. Now I paddled by, reassured to see that it was still there, as were the local harbor seals basking on Yellow's western spit, a favored haulout. I gave their loafing bar a wide berth so as not to disturb them.

By two in the afternoon I had bested a fifteen- to twenty-knot headwind across San

Juan Channel and entered Friday Harbor, the metropolis of the islands and a wonderful port of call. There were boats everywhere: sturdy whalers at the Friday Harbor labs of the University of Washington marine research station, graceful Yankee sloops, and stalwart Blanchard Seniors lying at anchor, their halyards drumming in the wind. An increasing number of big white boxy boats were busy depreciating at the town dock. In the middle of it all, the ferry *Evergreen State* rumbled to a stop to offload a hundred cars and hundreds of walk-on passengers, bicyclists, dogs, Rollerbladers, and kayakers. I threaded my way between piers, secured Boato among the rowboats, and sauntered into town.

A communion of pigeon guillemots (Cepphus columba) *adrift on President Channel.*

Friday Harbor is a village on a hill with a turn-of-the-century main street leading up from the water. It has a character both utilitarian and touristy. Amid the curio shops and real-estate agencies are small grocery and hardware stores, a movie theater, and a defiant tavern that is proud to let Budweiser neon proclaim its stand against gentrification. I sought out the Blue Dolphin cafe, the locals' greasy spoon, selected sections of the two- and three-day-old newspapers from a stack by the door (the Mariners had beat the Texas Rangers 18 to 9), and ordered a big breakfast. After a brief look at the real-estate prices and a stop at the grocery, I returned to the water and paddled east past Turn Island through Upright Channel, dodging the ferry and, turning west, rounded Shaw Island to land at tiny Blind Island.

En route I had passed a couple in a double kayak that in time beached alongside me. They were new to kayaking, a fact that became clear to me as they unstrapped their full-size cooler from atop their mid-deck—an unprecedented example of excessive deck gear. Middle-aged, they were without the common trappings of the Northwest outdoors type (no beards, ponytails, Tevas, T-shirts commemorating some gnarly event—not even any items of clothing from Patagonia!). As we unpacked, I learned they were from Seattle and they were on the Trail. But when I asked the man whether he was a member of the Washington Water Trails Association or used the state park annual pass, he said he didn't need to. "I let others pay for that," he said.

So I did. When I came to the pay station, I paid the fourteen dollars for the two of them, all the while chewing on whether this encounter constituted a sea-change in the culture of sea kayaking. In the nearly twenty years since I'd begun, I'd always found that the "new-to-sea-kayaking people" blended easily with the "people who already sea kayak," matching them in environmental ethics, morals, and T-shirts. Now I was sharing an island no bigger than a football field with a Manifest Destiny poster child.

That night it began to rain. I put up the tarp, and it stopped. I would have to try that again.

)
(
)

My friends Scott and Mary arrived at Spencer Spit State Park late in the afternoon. I helped carry their gear up the hill, following the water-trail signs to an old farmstead orchard, one of the nicest sites on the Trail. From our vantage point, we looked east across a spit encompassing a saltwater marsh. The point, almost touching Frost Island, was dotted with random beach walkers and marauding crows. Behind us stretched our island for the night, Lopez, the third largest, the flattest, and the least developed of the three major islands.

Mary and Scott at Spencer Spit, dry bags in tow.

The next morning we made for Orcas, the second largest and the most convoluted island of them all. We aimed toward Eastsound, a fjord with a bakery where we tried to buy an entire blueberry pie but failed (twenty-four hours' notice required) and so had to settle for cinnamon rolls and omelets. We then followed the ferry westbound between Shaw and Orcas, aiming to reach Jones Island in the middle of the afternoon. A mile off the western tip of Orcas, Jones, the island with the sunset camp I'd passed three days before, is a state marine park. There is a fine protected harbor with a pier on the north shore and a good open-meadow camping area with a fair beach on the south side. But it was the sunset camp, a small bight on the west shore with an eighty-foot-long beach, a fine madrona leafed out over a lone picnic table, and a trail-site sign, that was our goal.

As I scanned San Juan Channel, I caught the telltale flashes of distant kayak

Sea kayakers off Clark Island investigate pocket beaches.

*Kayakers and their kids arrive
at the Jones Island trail site.*

paddles. I stared in some disbelief at thirteen kayaks in three or four different parties, all converging on Jones. "Well," I told myself, "if you want to camp on your favorite spot you'd better get going." I called back to Mary and Scott to meet me on the far side and took off, paddling a sprint to the sunset camp.

The group coming from the direction of Yellow Island looked like a sea kayak guide trip, judging by the number of doubles and shepherding singles—too big a party for our destination. But the other group of five or six singles out from Orcas was fair game. I passed the double two strokes to their one. The singles were ahead of me—but they were not in a hurry. Mercifully, I did not have to paddle past them gunwale to gunwale, looking a plain fool. They dawdled at the south beach. I passed them a hundred yards off and slacked my pace, rounding a series of false points to the sunset camp with an easy stroke. Two kayaks on the beach and a family at the picnic table—there was room for all of us.

I pulled up on the fine pebble beach and, rummaging in the bow, came up with my tent and sleeping bag to anchor my preferred site. I said hello to the established campers and, just beyond their tents, staked our claim on a small point, flat and shaded.

By the time I returned to the beach, the six single kayakers had arrived, with Mary and Scott closely following. They settled in above the beach in what I thought was the last possible site. But as sunset approached a couple of women arrived and, without a word or glance to any of us, carried their gear *and* their kayaks up past us to camp on a fragile grassland knob. That night there were thirteen kayaks at the sunset camp and thirty-seven kayaks in all on Jones Island. The human-powered watercraft paradise was filled to capacity.

Were we kayakers simply becoming too many, too diverse, too damaging? There has been a long-standing assumption within the sea kayaking community that the sport is low impact. And compared to hiking, mountain biking, snowmobiling, or driving off-road vehicles, it is. We don't use fossil fuel; we camp on beaches, a practice that has a lighter impact on the land (especially if we do without fires!) than bedding down on the upland. We consider ourselves as a group, with the exception of the couple at Blind Island, environmentally and ethically conscious. But in the spring and summer months at Jones and other favorite spots in the San Juans, we are clearly overgrazing our camping areas.

And what effect do our numbers have on the resident wildlife communities? I managed to keep the seals on their Yellow Island haulout when I passed by, but how many times that day did another group get a bit too close and force them into the water? The kayak and the canoe are very effective hunting tools. We can go where no one else can—and easily frighten the pigeon guillemots from their rookeries, the kingfishers from their perches, the bears from the beaches in the process.

Our relationship with the San Juan islanders isn't in the best of health either. We are the first waterborne folk with sufficient numbers to significantly impinge upon the domain of the waterfront property owner. Regrettably, some sea kayakers who need to relieve themselves after a two- or three-hour crossing see a beach and paddle in. This is not a good way to meet a San Juan Island resident. Paddlers camping overnight above the tideline on posted, private beaches caused a group of Shaw Island property owners to band together to buy the most convenient launch site in the islands, specifically to prevent sea kayakers from launching there.

GOSSIP ISLAND

Conservation biologist Terry DoMico started out searching for the prickly pear cactus (Opuntia fragilis) on Jones Island, in an effort to save this unusual plant from local extinction. Eventually, however, he expanded his goal from preserving one plant to safeguarding whole habitats. "I realized we have no understanding of what the natural wealth of this county is, so I began searching for priority habitats to protect the biodiversity of the San Juans." As a result, Terry discovered 1.5-acre Gossip Island, located on the south side of Stuart Island and owned by Washington State Parks. Supporting a tiny grassland habitat—characterized by native bunch grasses, camas, chocolate lilies, and a rare lance-leafed sedum—it's a surprising relic of the Puget Prairie Complex, the reigning environment of the region over 4,000 years ago. When he informed the state parks system about his exciting find, Terry also discovered that Gossip Island was designated to become a Cascadia Marine Trail campsite. He petitioned to make it a Natural Protected Area. Now you can visit Gossip Island, but the trail site is across the way on Stuart.

Suddenly we seem to be the greatest threat since the invasion of the Californians, silly as that may sound. But that doesn't deal with the issue. Clearly we have to do a better job of educating and communicating with both kayakers and island residents.

Zoologist Jane Lubchenko held up a big purple sea star. "*Pisaster ochraceus*," she said, returning it gently to its rock and nabbing a smaller and less showy gray-green competitor: "*Leptasterias hexactis*." Both of these sea stars, when not being measured by marine researchers, are predators of the barnacles, limpets, and mussels that live in San Juan Island's Lonesome Cove. Jane and her husband, marine biologist Bruce Menge, both

CLEAVING THE SURFACE

professors at Oregon State University, had returned to Lonesome Cove thirty years after Bruce's initial survey to reassess the range, abundance, and relations of predator and prey.

Meeting Jane and Bruce had been sheer chance. I had left Mary and Scott at Jones, they to return to civilization on the incoming tide, and I to catch the ebb. As I paddled San Juan Island's northwest shore, the sight of two booted people hunting through the intertidal zone with clipboard and quadrat (a meter-square measuring device) caught my attention and pulled me into the quiet cove. This was one of Bruce's twelve study sites encircling San Juan Island, and he told me he was finding "a greatly reduced abundance of not just sea stars but also predatory snails, limpets, and chitons, and in some places a complete disappearance" of some species. I examined one particularly robust survivor, a *Pisaster* wreathed in seaweed. This relative of the sand dollar and the sea urchin had caught my eye not only for its somewhat lonely existence but for the way it

Rosario Strait in a mirror calm, with Orcas Island and Mount Constitution three miles distant.

Dr. Jane Lubchenko at a research site in the San Juan Islands.

molded its body to an offshore rock.

As I left the cove and entered Spieden Channel, I reflected on what the original richness of the Puget Sound and San Juan regions must have been like. The straits, the Sound, the estuaries and rivers, the land itself and what lived upon it—all must have paused, in an annual collective geobiological holding of breath, as the first of the salmon nosed in from sea to stream, from salt water to fresh, from migration to spawning redd. Beginning in February the spring chinook, or king salmon, arrived; in July and August, the sockeye (red) salmon and a second run of chinook; in September and October, the coho (silver) and, in odd-numbered years, the pinks (humpback); and, at the onset of winter, the chum or dog salmon. Millions upon millions of fish found every possible gravel bed on every possible stream, weighing down the land like the aquatic advance of a redd-defending, milt-squirting, egg-laying, life-creating glacier. Today the National Marine Fisheries Service is struggling with the task of designating specific Puget Sound "stocks" as either threatened or endangered (a stock is a type of salmon that spawns in one particular river). Eight stocks are now extinct.

With my kayak, my direct contact with the natural environment had increased over the years, but my random encounters with wildlife—of salmon jumping close aboard or harlequin ducks in sudden flight—had decreased. The wild was being whittled away in my lifetime, yet Puget Sound residents argue about reduced recreational-fishing limits and the inalienable rights of the landowner. Meanwhile, the sea

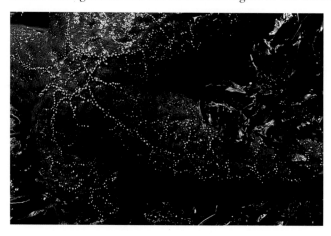

A purple sea star (Pisaster ochraceus) *in Lonesome Cove.*

stars and wild salmon are quietly being denied habitat, weakened by pollution, or fished to the brink of extinction. The pattern of encroachment is now reaching the largest predators: the orcas are rumored to be spreading out in search of scarcer prey.

Sockeye salmon (Oncorhynchus nerka) *struggle in the webbing of a seine net.*

ROCHE HARBOR

Nestled into the western corner of San Juan Island, deep in a protected bay, is an establishment rare in the Northwest: the 112-year-old resort known as Roche Harbor. The quaintly formal twenty-room Hotel de Haro has defied fire and developer alike to set the standard of style, if not amenities, in this rapidly developing archipelago. Built atop the remains of an 1840s Hudson's Bay Company outpost, the hotel is not state of the art. Many of the twenty rooms share baths— but the President's Suite, so named for a visiting Theodore Roosevelt in 1906 and 1907, has an exquisite view to the west. Surrounding the two-story structure are 4,000 acres of forest, meadow, old cabins, and—more recently— condos. The garden is trellised and profuse, and the sun-drenched restaurant deck has a perpetual waiting list. The marina is ship-shape, with public showers, a grocery and espresso stand, and visiting boats that tend to be large and impeccable. It is a place both attractive and ostentatious, one part yacht club, one part town.

San Juan Island's southwestern corner cuts into the Strait of Juan de Fuca like the prow of a great ship. Around it, the remnants of the once-great salmon runs of Cascadia swim toward their ancestral streams. At Lime Kiln Point, the majority of the Fraser River run (British Columbia's largest single river spawn) turns north, following the current into Haro Strait. Centuries ago *Orcinus orca*, the killer whale, discovered that the salmon schooled here off San Juan, Henry, and Stuart Islands, and they moved in, in extended matriarchal families known as pods, to feed from spring through summer on each salmon species moving through. Their successors are now the resident orcas, known as the J, K, and L pods, which daily draw a host of devout whale watchers to Lime Kiln. Families, photographers, newlyweds, people from all walks of life and levels of environmental awareness command the rocks around the lighthouse, while powerboaters and kayakers dawdle as they wait for a glimpse of the "blackfish," the dominant mammal of the ocean's food chain. And most days from mid-June through mid-September, they're not disappointed.

Lime Kiln has become so popular that for the past eight summers Bob Otis, a psychology professor from Ripon College, has migrated with his students in tow from Ripon, Wisconsin, to the point to study the interaction of orcas and orca watchers. Using the automated lighthouse as an office, Bob and his assistants continually monitor the radio and the horizon for word or sight of the whales. When a pod arrives off Lime Kiln Point, it is announced not by the sight of the great black dorsal fins of the 10,000-pound bulls but by a flotilla of powerboats, sailboats, Zodiacs, and commercial whale-watching vessels shadowing the orcas as they hunt, rest, and play. Once the whales enter the one-by-one-half-mile study area, Bob tracks them with a theodolite or rangefinder to fix their

The Hotel de Haro: host to seafaring guests at Roche Harbor, San Juan Island, for more than a hundred years.

location as the trailing watercraft are counted and the behavior of both whales and humans is filmed.

But not at five-thirty in the morning. Knowing that Bob's daily period of observation mimics boaters' hours, nine to five, I chose to meet the orcas by myself, unobserved, as the sun crested over San Juan Island's Mount Dallas.

Off Lime Kiln the morning was beautiful: no wind as yet and only two salmon fishermen trolling west of me, their conversation a distinct murmur from a mile away. I let Boato drift with the flood sweeping me back toward Kelp Reef and D'Arcy Island as I scanned the horizon. The boat lazily spun in the current, pointing me now toward the hazy Olympics, now toward Victoria and its offshore islands. Every once in awhile I would paddle upstream to regain my station a half mile west of the point. With no orcas in sight, I was hopeful but not overly optimistic.

Each of the past three years, I had come here hoping to encounter orcas. I wanted to observe the whales from a kayak rather than from a more versatile but intrusive powerboat, and I wasn't anxious to share the moment with the usual entourage of whale watchers. So now, for the fourth year, I floated in anticipation, paddling back to Lime Kiln and then drifting some more. Around 7 A.M. the sounds of sharp, quick exhaling and inhaling alerted me to a pair of Dall's porpoises; they passed at a distance, little dorsal fins surfacing in the blink of an eye. A few more salmon fishermen arrived by eight. By nine I'd had too much sun and paddled into Deadman Bay, immediately south of Lime Kiln, for breakfast and a chat with Bob Otis.

Bob was a professor in summer mode, approachable and generous with his time when whale watchers and journalists sought him out. Scanning the sweeping view of Juan de Fuca and Haro Straits as he talked, he said the

Bob Otis sights his theodolite on an orca subpod heading north, in Haro Strait.

current orca population was about ninety-one, including the J pod (nineteen orcas), K pod (eighteen), and L pod (fifty-four). Four to five times a year they form a superpod off Lime Kiln; but for the most part the pods remain separate, with one to five pods passing the point daily.

Over the summers Bob has counted thousands of boats and conversed with hundreds of watchers onshore. And over the years he has seen a whale-watching ethic form within both groups: "The vast majority of boats are polite in the human sense of the word—they simply run parallel to the whales. . . . There is a sort of sense of responsibility, a common feeling toward protecting them." (This is particularly noticeable, he says, with the land-bound orca watchers, who vocally deride any boater's overenthusiastic action.) In 1990 the average number of boats and kayaks in the study area during a whale sighting was 4.4; by 1997 the average was 26.0. The greatest number of boats following any one pod through the study boundaries was 107 during the 1996 Fourth of July holiday, an almost incredible number.

| Orcinus orca.

Naturally, my next question was about kayakers and whether he remembered any particular kayaker-orca encounters. "Well," he said, "there was the time when *you* were bumped by an orca." I looked at him as if in shock, but he was right. Like a victim of amnesia, I had completely forgotten that three years ago, under the watchful eye of Bob and his students, I was bumped by a whale. Now I remembered being shoved firmly sideways, but I could not remember the approach, the whale, or the aftermath.

Bob noted my embarrassment and said, "You weren't being aggressive; you were just out from the kelp line," meaning that I had not blocked the whale's path, as some kayakers tend to do. "A very common kayak behavior is what we call ambushing: to

move directly out in front of the pod. . . . Kayakers also raft up [sit gunwale to gunwale] and often deliberately drift out in front of a pod. We also see what appears to be chasing, but it is a hopeless chase," as orcas, even when asleep, travel at five knots or better. Yet in all his years of monitoring boats and orcas, Bob has yet to find evidence that the boats harass the whales.

I asked him what changes he'd noticed in behavior of the whales. "Things are changing now. The whales are not as clumped up as they used to be. Today they were spread out over a mile or two. Our most reasonable hypothesis for this new behavior is there are fewer salmon. A more efficient way to hunt is to spread out."

From Deadman Bay I prepared to catch a tide that would take me along the southern shore of San Juan Island to my next trail site. As I paddled, I felt deeply worried. That we should disturb our own environment to the extent that we lose what we are most proud of seems now a distinct possibility—first *Pisasters*, then Salmonidae, now *Orcinus orca*. Brock Evans, head of the Endangered Species Act Coalition and a longtime crusader for habitat and wildlife, has said, "Puget Sound could be dying the death of a thousand cuts—no single one fatal, but added together, the consequences could be just as tragic and just as fatal." And with that depressing thought, I pushed off the beach and paddled smack into a pod of orcas.

First I saw the boats: two clumps of them, moving toward me very slowly. Then I saw the brief plumes of whale breaths and the stately rise and fall of orca dorsal fins. I stopped paddling and waited as the line—more than a mile wide—of orca bulls, cows, and calves moved toward me. There was no getting out of the way. With half a mile between us I began mentally to time their movements: a pattern of three short dives and then a longer one of four to five minutes. They were either feeding or resting, I thought, as one or two whales broke from the line to circle back and then resume their journey toward me. At a thousand feet the pod took a deep dive and two smaller whales, either moms or good-size youngsters, and one full-size bull seemed headed in my direction. I was a little nervous as the seconds clicked away, my eyes sweeping in an arc across the Strait of Juan de Fuca as the orcas echolocated beneath me.

And then there he was: the bull, his fin silently cleaving the surface of the sea not more than forty feet away. Then his head and body appeared, as if encased in glass. With a loud exhalation and a quieter, almost human inhalation, the orca passed beside me and continued on about his life.

Beyond the Lime Kiln Point lighthouse is the Strait of Juan de Fuca and, thirty miles farther, the Olympic Peninsula.

The rain that had followed me down the straits from Lime Kiln Point caught up with me at the Griffin Bay trail site on San Juan Island. It rained night into morning, and morning into a sky so resolutely gray, so universally wet that I thought of author Tom Robbins's comment on our Puget Sound existence: "Sunbeams are a lot like tourists: intruding where they don't belong, promoting noise and forced activity, faking a shallow

FROM RAIN TO RESONANCE

cheerfulness, dumb little cameras slung around their necks. Raindrops, on the other hand—introverted, feral, buddhistically cool—behave as if they live here. Which of course, they do."

I bent beneath the wet tarp and prepared breakfast. The tide paused, and in an hour I slipped Boato back through Cattle Pass and into the Strait of Juan de Fuca. Riding the outflow of the morning ebb, I found I was keeping company with a lone minke whale. Like the elephant seal, the twenty-nine-foot, nine-ton minke is a solitary sea mammal, a fellow traveler in a meditative rainscape. He surfaced three times, just showing his shark-finned black back before we went our separate ways.

I stayed to the rocky, low-cliffed coast of Lopez Island, heading east, fighting the back eddies toward Point Colville and the entrance to Rosario Strait. This was one of the finest coastlines on the Trail and my favorite in the San Juans. It is known for its off-

An oil-soaked common murre (Uria aalge), *a victim of the sinking of the* Tenyo Maru *off Cape Flattery.*

shore fishing and diving and its landscaped feel: a meadowed shore with a forest of juniper and fir set back from the salt spray—a setting for an Andrew Wyeth painting. But today was a day for minimalists, the color sucked from the sea and sky, the drizzle in between so monochromatic there was no horizon until a random pigeon guillemot surfaced to lend perspective.

At the last possible point of land, I turned across the growing ebb tide from Rosario Strait and began the eight-mile crossing to Whidbey Island. There were two tankers exiting the strait, and I stopped to let them go by. The *Palmstar Poppy*, an Asian tanker,

With "tarpness," the kitchen at the Griffin Bay trail site stays dry!

was loaded with oil and under the escort of two Crowley Maritime tugs. Their job, by order of the state of Washington, was to aid this tanker should it lose power or steering. With one tug to port and another to starboard, the convoy steamed westward, one visible victory in the past quarter century of the fight to protect Puget Sound.

The *Palmstar Poppy* represents only one of more than eight hundred tankers to pass through Washington waters in 1997, only one of the 20,000 ships that navigate the straits annually. "And that's not including the movement within the Sound—not counting the ferries or the tugs and barges delivering fuel oil locally," says Fred Felleman, an environmental consultant and Northwest director of Ocean Advocates. "The most important issue is spill prevention. Once the oil is out of the ship, with the currents in these waters we'd be lucky to clean up 10 to 50 percent, even under ideal conditions."

I well knew what he was talking about, having myself been a witness to the infamous Anacortes oil spill of 1971, when tankermen aboard the barge UT17 accidentally

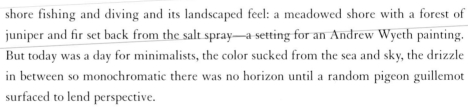

The Arco Anchorage *is contained by booms after spilling 239,000 gallons of crude oil into Puget Sound.*

pumped 230,000 gallons of diesel fuel into Padilla Bay. The oil slick plumed out through Rosario Strait, past Point Colville and toward Smith Island, choking the life out of the intertidal community and the resident seabirds around Guemes Channel and Cypress and southern Lopez Islands.

At the time of that spill, Washington State had a strong set of environmentally astute leaders, notably Governor Daniel Evans and Senators Warren Magnuson and Henry Jackson. Together with the newly established state Department of Ecology and numerous academic and environmental groups, they began to draft legislation and defend court cases that resulted in a series of state laws more stringent than the federal laws combating oil pollution. The 1971 Washington Oil Pollution Act established unlimited liability for oil spills, provided for cleanup capability, and specifically clarified that the discharge of any oil into state waters was illegal. In 1975 the Washington legislature passed the Washington Tanker Safety Act, which prohibited supertankers of a certain size from entering the Sound and required escort tugs for smaller tankers. (The U.S. Supreme Court struck down the supertanker ban, but Senator Magnuson later reestablished it via new legislation in 1979.) And the outcry following the *Exxon Valdez* tragedy in 1989 allowed the state Department of Ecology to resurrect,

Under tug escort, the Palmstar Poppy *begins a course change for open sea.*

pass, and fund a comprehensive spill prevention, preparedness, and response program that the legislature had originally defeated in the 1970s.

At Buoy R not more than seven miles seaward of our meeting, 74 miles before the open sea, and 115 miles before the *Palmstar Poppy* will be clear of the Olympic Coast National Marine Sanctuary, the escort tugs leave the ship. Should this tanker then run amok while transiting the straits, a "tug of convenience" will attempt a rescue. Washington's spill prevention program, still considered one of the best in the nation, is now scarcely more reliable than a lottery.

The twelve-foot ebb I first met at Rosario Strait now began toying with me as I made the crossing to Whidbey Island. Any thought of staying at the Joseph Whidbey State Park site north of my track was literally swept away as I now paddled simply to make landfall. On my right lay distant Smith Island. A U.S. Fish and Wildlife Preserve and a geology lesson in erosion (one of its abandoned Coast Guard buildings hangs precariously, just half a house, over the western cliff), Smith is the most isolated island in greater Puget Sound. I did not want to go there, even to see if that ruin still stood, but for an hour I seemed to get closer and closer. Because of the tide pull, each attempt to gain on Whidbey put me closer to Smith. Finally, I was able to paddle beyond the main stem of the tide and into the shallows of a lonely Whidbey shore.

Spread before me lay a dramatic seascape—cliffs rising abruptly from a flat sand beach to a tree-fringed summit of three hundred or more feet. As I turned Boato to parallel this wall of glacial till, I could see it stretching for miles, a near-naked wilderness of talus vegetation and an occasional barnacle-encrusted erratic. After a brief, wet stop for the last of my peanut butter supply, I settled in for six miles of riding the kelp line to a break in this wall of sand at Fort Ebey State Park and a then as-yet-to-be-created trail site. My Washington Water Trails guidebook described the approach to Ebey as "easy gravel beach." But that assessment had not been made in a two-foot minus tide. The beach at Fort Ebey today was in fact a forty-foot-wide band of seaweed-coated bowling balls. I paddled from one end of the park to the other, searching for a better landing and finding none; finally, I gingerly brought my kayak in. I put up a tarp amid snowberries and hawthorn bushes and then the rain, steady for almost twenty-four

A long-abandoned Coast Guard residence teeters on the west-facing bluff of Smith Island.

*Low tide's bowling-ball beach
at Fort Ebey State Park.*

hours, relented enough for me to reconnoiter this decommissioned World War II coastal defense battery.

At one time Fort Ebey had sixteen-inch guns capable of lobbing one-ton shells twenty-five miles down the Strait of Juan de Fuca. I could see why this bluff was picked to guard our cities. Today the guns are gone but the parapet remains, and the view from it, high above the beach, is all-encompassing. I could see down Admiralty Inlet to Point No Point, up Rosario toward Vancouver, and down the Strait of Juan de Fuca in a direct line to Russia's Kamchatka Peninsula. But the focus of my attention was the pattern of currents and winds that stretched between me and my next destination, the town of Port Townsend. I could see the shoals and banks, the patches of standing waves and calmer waters, and filed them in my memory for tomorrow's six-mile crossing, one of the toughest paddles of the entire trip.

I awoke at 4 A.M. to the unmistakable sound of surf. During the night the wind had shifted to the northwest, driving in the swells from the Pacific and funneling them down the strait to beat against this weathered seascape. The tide notwithstanding, I had been lucky to arrive the day before in an unusual calm; now it sounded as if I'd be lucky to leave.

Loading the odds and ends of camping into my duffel bags, I trundled through the forest and onto the beach. The waves were averaging two to three feet, four at the highest. But they were close-ordered, steep and dumping. (When a beach is steep, the waves do not feel the bottom until very near the shore, where they break late or "dump" in a sudden wall of water with little or no swash or runout afterward.) I spotted a slight break in the waves, a small undertow perhaps, that left a low spot in the oncoming wave trains. I retrieved Boato from the beach grass and set her down, pointed toward the Pacific. The roof of cloud that had inundated Western Washington was sliding eastward, its trailing edge a sharp diagonal line over the strait. Beyond it I saw a morning-blue sky, the sunrise warming the Olympic Mountains and the San Juans, and whitecaps—a sea of whitecaps—where I intended to go.

I pulled Boato down into the wet sand of the swash zone and jumped in, trying to get my spray skirt on before the next wave came and took me seaward. Instead it turned me broadside. I hopped out and pulled the kayak back a bit, realigned it, and reentered. The next wave was not enough to float me. With my skirt secure, I poled the bow around with my paddle and watched as the next big set of waves arrived; in theory, the last big wave would take me out to meet the smaller waves that followed. First one wave and then another rode up under my fully loaded kayak. With each I levered forward with my fists plunged into the sand. The next wave looked big enough, so I grabbed my paddle as the outwash skidded me down the beach into the face of the next cold, green wave. I folded forward with my paddle blade flat on the deck as the wave hit, momen-

The surf, the tide, and the distant Olympics in morning sunlight upon my departure for Port Townsend.

tarily staggering me. A set of quick strokes and I regained momentum and sliced through the second wave, taking water but gaining speed. Cresting the third, Boato went momentarily airborne, slamming back on the flat of the sea with a pleasant smack. In the meantime I felt the shock of fifty-four-degree salt water trickling in. Quickly I got my bearings and, remembering what I had surmised from atop the bluff, paddled away from my Port Townsend destination, heading west into a miserably confused sea.

The slack ebb had been at four in the morning; it was now five. I should have been riding the incoming tide along with a ten-knot wind, but the last of the ebb came out of Admiralty Inlet to ambush me. Ordered ranks of seas and currents met off Point Partridge in wave-to-wave combat. It was fun; it was scary. Every stroke was deliberate as I strove to find workable pathways through the sea of whitecaps.

Finally paddling clear of the chaos, I began to realize a new condition, a sea kayaker's version of what whitewater kayakers call being "maytagged" (a reference to the rotating water or wave, reminiscent of a washing machine, that can trap a kayaker). Triangulating on Point Hudson, Point Wilson on my right shoulder and the high bluff

Schooners, sloops, and a ketch lie in the Point Hudson boat basin, Port Townsend.

of Marrowstone Point on my left, I sensed I was being drawn into a circular current while paddling toward the port. I then made a ninety-degree course change, and in no time I was a mile below Port Townsend, off Point Wilson with its finely shaped lighthouse. Once inside the shearing curve of the point, I caught another eddy heading toward the town proper and let Boato drift past the soon-to-be trail site above the beach. In time this site will become a major jumping-off point for the Cascadia Marine Trail, but today I paddled past it, intent on a motel, a shower, and a regrouping, for I was going to spend the Fourth of July in Port Townsend.

One of my favorite American towns, Port Townsend is a place of boatyards, long-bar taverns, pulp-mill payrolls, and nearly 9,000 souls. It is an

Mount Baker frames the Point Wilson lighthouse at Fort Worden State Park.

Two Puget Sound locals: David George Gordon and the geoduck (Panopea abrupta).

eccentric town in that many of its residents decided to live here on the spur of the moment—as soon as they saw it laid out before them from the crest of State Highway 113. They saw a compact town straddling a small peninsula, the original 1890s business district fronting Port Townsend bay to the south, the residential neighborhoods neatly platted above, with Fort Worden, a Spanish-American War–era coastal defense base, claiming the higher ground on the north shore. When the town was denied its entrepreneurial dream of becoming a major rail terminus, it promptly became a backwater in time and pace, a turn-of-the-century artifact. Today it is a town surrounded by population centers but somehow unscathed by it all. No wonder it has attracted utopians, iconoclasts, poets, and eccentrics.

Among these painters, jugglers, plank-steaming mariners, and dulcimer makers lives nature writer David George Gordon, who, with his wife, Mari, and their daughter, Julia, seems perfectly settled in Port Townsend, this city that never was. David came west from Chicago in 1981 and met Mari in Seattle; they stayed there for a decade, building their careers and raising Julia. But in time, said David, "I became urbaned to death and decided if I was a nature writer, I wanted more access to nature. We started looking at ways of living outside the city. We rented a place in Port Townsend, and we liked it." Mari found work at Centrum, an ever-evolving arts and education program at Fort Worden, now a Washington state park. The talent and entertainment that Centrum brought to Port Townsend were a cultural nutrient trap into which the Gordons lodged. They rafted into an 1893 blue-collar Victorian with old-glaze windowpanes and a chicken coop out back.

Cultural necessities, economic realities, social climates: all of these played a role in

From the west beach at Fort Worden, Whidbey Island's bluffs and, farther west, the San Juans and Vancouver Island.

their decision to settle down here, but underneath it all was the romance of water—Puget Sound. "I like the fact that as a point of land, Port Townsend is sticking out into Puget Sound. . . . It's perched like an eagle's nest at the confluence of three bodies of water. That's why everyone's here," David told me. "I joke about former Atlantians—there are some of us who are happiest in a boat. We are water people, just as there are mountain people, desert people, some who are into dirt. But for water people, this place resonates."

That evening, as pop-bottle rockets arched onto the roofs of old chicken coops throughout Port Townsend, David's remarks resonated loudly within me. With an optimism born of a liberal arts education, I sensed that a large and potentially powerful force for the environment is moving into place. Never before has a civilization had such freedom of movement to act on these innate currents of our individual beings. Water people are moving toward the water, mountain people are heading for the hills, and we are creating in the basins of Puget Sound, Georgia Strait, and Oregon's Willamette River—what planners call "Cascadia"—quorums with the strength and qualifications to enable the science, fund the restoration, and provide the volunteers to see that the health of the watersheds and coastal tidelands is protected. David George Gordon is a nature-writing, child-rearing, Port Townsend–residing example of this promise. And though it was tempting to consider how well I could renovate a hundred-year-old Victorian house on the hill above Water Street, I had to finish this trip on my own waterfront, where I feel most strongly my own sense of place—Seattle.

RAIN SHADOWS

During the first week of July, a rain shower off the southern end of Lopez Island is a rare event. In notoriously wet Western Washington, the San Juan Islands have the least precipitation. Twenty inches of rain or less fall on southern Lopez, the western side of Whidbey, Port Townsend, Port Angeles, and the waters in between. The principle reason is the Olympic Mountains. Not more than fifty miles away, the western slopes of these six- to eight-thousand-foot summits accept up to 240 inches of rain a year from the fronts blowing in from the Gulf of Alaska. What is left as the front blows eastward falls into what meteorologists call the "rain shadow." Within this rain shadow are retirement communities and cactus, Naval air stations, and three hundred days of sunshine.

The trail sites within the rain shadow are Fort Worden and Fort Flagler on the Olympic Peninsula; Bowman Bay, Fort Ebey, and Joseph Whidbey State Park on Whidbey Island; and Griffin Bay and James Island in the San Juans.

The pasture beside David Gordon's house, Port Townsend.

The delightful serenity of the weather greatly aided the beautiful scenery that was now presented; the surface of the sea was perfectly smooth, and the country before us exhibited every thing that bounteous nature could be expected to draw into one point of view. . . . A picture so pleasing could not fail to call to our remembrance certain delightful and beloved situations in Old England.

—Captain George Vancouver, in his journal

A GPS FOR THE SOUL

Vancouver, the consummate world traveler (he circumnavigated the globe with English navigator James Cook in 1772–75 and 1776–80), was writing the Sound's real-estate ad, its economic forecast, and its tourist brochure. The date was May 2, 1792, as his ship, the HMS *Discovery*, rode at anchor five miles from the harbor he would name Port Townshend. Vancouver had another 1,184 days under sail before he would land at Shannon, Ireland, on September 13, 1795. I had just two days "at sea" remaining—just two days to consider what these past four hundred miles meant before I landed at the foot of Washington Street in Seattle.

It was a breezy and sunny midday as I raced the sloops making for the Port Townsend canal. I had chosen the protected passage down Port Townsend Bay, staying close to Marrowstone and then Indian Island. Point No Point was at least four hours

The tug Shelly Foss *glides past Seattle's container ships, cranes, and office towers.*

distant, and the tide would turn against me in midpaddle. But on this downwind, down-current, quiet water passage, it was easy to relax and think about my journey through Puget Sound.

The Cascadia Marine Trail had given me the Sound itself: the straits and channels, the marshes, the rock gardens, the water, the life—an ocean of natural and human intricacies continually unfolding along my track. And from within my small, capable kayak I had enjoyed a perspective unlike that from any beach-house front window, whirling jet ski, or ambling state ferry. I was truly *within* this massive estuary, my progress so slow that I could experience geologic time, my passage so close I could witness a kingfisher's lair, my "footprint" so small I was welcomed by the neighborhood of Point No Point. And oh, how I was drawn to that.

Puget Sound, Mount Rainier, and Seattle from Kingston's Appletree Cove.

When I approached Point No Point, I had an audience of fishermen and strollers on the beach, making me realize I too had a cameo role in the Point No Point tableau. Once through the sheer line, I paddled through the smooth-as-glass current surging around the tip of the point. Fifteen–twenty quick, sharp strokes, and the friction on my hull fell away; I shot forward into the calm water of the south beach. I hunted for the place where Carey and I had set up camp two weeks before, and nudged Boato up the sand.

With Mount Rainier glowing in the southern distance, and a dwindling number of "hellos" and "fine days" passing by, I scrounged in the food bag for dinner. Up around the lighthouse the sunset silhouetted the fishermen in a big wide sky, and a burr-headed, big-cheeked boy who looked much as I had when I was nine clambered along the riprap between the beach and the

Buddy Graff rock-hops on the riprap of Point No Point.

Coast Guard light station. A sailboat fighting the worst of the current was hugging the beach just the way I had done. Beyond everything, the mountains to the east spoke of a good summer snowpack: White Horse, Three Fingers, and Mount Pilchuck.

With my first bite of dinner I realized that sand, the curse of all beach cooking, had found its way into my food. I gritted my way through my meal and the grand sunset, reflecting that I was twenty-four miles from home and the hardscrabble business dealings of a freelancer. If I were going to make sense of my voyage in the next twenty hours, I would need a sort of global positioning satellite, a GPS for my soul: You are here in Puget Sound: 48° 54' 42" N / 122° 54' 27" W, four feet above mean high tide, and what are you going to do about it?

One inescapable fact had confronted me on this trip: The life of the Sound, the straits, the islands is in serious trouble. On the surface the Puget Sound region is one of the most beautiful places on earth. Yet 40 percent of the Sound's shellfish are contaminated with fecal coliform bacteria and pulp-mill waste; 70 percent of the original estuaries no longer exist; and the lingcod, rockfish, pollock, and hake stocks are either sharply declining, in critical condition, or nearly extinct. In the straits the wild salmon, the emblematic species of our region, is being fought over by American and Canadian fishermen—who are "solving" their disputes by outfishing each other for the scarce resource. Meanwhile, 3.1 million central Puget Sounders are bracing for an estimated one million more neighbors by 2020, a 35 percent increase.

A PUGET SOUND DESIDERATUM

My hope in writing this book is to create an understanding of and a desire to preserve Puget Sound.

From the tiniest diatom to the largest corporation, we are all in this together. But diatoms don't volunteer for salmon stream clean-ups. It is we who live here who must realize the repercussions of our actions and take responsibility. Seemingly minor decisions can improve our water quality: using unbleached paper products, avoiding toxic fertilizers and pesticides, or planting a tree. Developers and home owners should create neighborhoods that embrace and protect habitat and minimize sprawl. Foresters must see the proverbial forest through the trees, while fishermen must recognize the wisdom in self-imposed limits. Farmers should work with nature to rejuvenate the watersheds. The maritime community should demand of themselves every safeguard to prevent oil spills in Northwest waters. Industries need to be accountable for their impact on the environment, and work creatively and decisively to end pollution. And we who enjoy the waters of Puget Sound—kayakers, fishermen, campers, guides—must give back as willing volunteers.

Maybe then, local governments and voters will support the protection of Puget Sound with good laws, good science, and generous funding. And all who live in the Puget Sound basin will have the courage to see that this is our heritage, our legacy, and our soul.

To deal with this litany of environmental miseries, we have about six hundred agencies, organizations, foundations, tribes, industries, and individuals dedicated to Puget Sound. They raise money, give money, fight bad legislation, clean up after

The legacy, the resource, the environment: a pulp and paper mill on Commencement Bay.

industry, reclaim streams, and educate the rest of us: Adopt a Beach, Cascade Designs, the Squaxin Tribe, the Seattle Audubon Society's Hazel Wolf, the Washington Department of Fish and Wildlife, the Bullitt Foundation, Wild Olympic Salmon, artist/educator Tony Angell, Chums of Barker Creek, software philanthropist Doug Walker, the Environmental Protection Agency, Long Live the Kings, Kelp Krawlers, B. J. Cummings of the Puget Soundkeeper Alliance, the Washington Wildlife and Recreation Program, and Trout Scouts, to name just a few. And then there is Kathy Fletcher and the People for Puget Sound.

Kathy Fletcher has fought for Puget Sound in business (as Seattle City Light's director of environmental affairs), in state government (as chair and director of the Puget Sound Water Quality Authority), and now as executive director of the nonprofit People for Puget Sound. As the head of the Puget Sound Water Quality Authority, she helped produce a management plan for Puget Sound in a year and a half. But when it came time to implement it, certain interest groups, including Boeing, were unwilling to accept it. And when the Water Quality Authority was up for reauthorization and re-funding before the legislature, lawmakers responded to these interest groups by pulling the teeth out of the agency. Kathy then founded People for Puget Sound "to mobilize the constituents, the kids, the grownups, to lobby in the legislature and in Congress. We are going to industry and business, talking to them about improving the way they produce their products—we are working at all levels because it is going to take all of that. . . . Part of our job is to help people connect to whatever it is about Puget Sound that motivates them. Get them to follow something specific, local, or compelling."

Danger on the Hylebos waterway, an Environmental Protection Agency Superfund site, at the Port of Tacoma.

Most of us who live between the mountains are so distant from the Sound that it has become an obstacle or a barrier rather than a habitat, highway, or heritage. We glimpse it through the high-rises, stew in our cars waiting for a ferry, and say we love it. Everyone should paddle, row, or day-sail the Cascadia Marine Trail; then maybe we would all have the proper respect for and commitment to the greater Puget Sound. After twenty-six days of getting wet in it, not only do you love it, you are willing to fight for it. The hope of the founders of the Cascadia Marine Trail is that those who travel through the Sound and the San Juans by human power will return with an affection for where they have been and a pride in having gotten there on their own that is sufficient to make them work to preserve it.

At 5:30 A.M. on my final day's paddle, I rechecked the Seattle tides for July 6, my thumb running across the line in the tidebook:

4:05 A.M.–3.5 feet; 9:35 A.M.–8.7 feet; 3:39 P.M.–1.4 feet; 10:33 P.M.–12.4 feet.

By 10:33 P.M.–12.4 feet, I hoped to be comfortably asleep in my own bed. I let that motivation be my breakfast as I hurried my gear into the kayak and launched off the shallow southern side of Point No Point. As I looked back, I committed myself to helping Washington Water Trails establish a trail site here at Point No Point. With a satisfied sense of closure, I let my bow enter the power of the new tide and pointed up Sound for Seattle.

Admiralty Inlet was blessed with as quiet a morning as one could hope for. There was a four- to five-knot north wind noiselessly traveling with me, and nothing but blue sky overhead. Knowing that in seven miles a good breakfast and a pay phone could be had in Kingston, I paddled with the current west of midchannel, then cut toward the town and the beach. I marched up the hill and, after putting in my order for a western omelet, called my girlfriend Maggie with my ETA. With seventeen miles of paddling against an outgoing tide, I estimated a three o'clock arrival at the foot of Washington Street. Then I settled in for breakfast and the anticipated baseball scores: Seattle had bested Texas again (and would go on to its first American League West championship).

By noon the wind was whitecapping the Sound. Boats were everywhere, bound for one port or another or just squirreling about at the end of this hot, clear, memorable

Fourth of July weekend. I used the boats that crisscrossed my path to maintain my speed, setting courses to intercept sailboats tacking down Sound or varying my course slightly to draw close to powerboats. I skinned by two sloops racing each other, their lee decks awash. A Foss tug running light (without a tow) around Magnolia for her ship canal berth gave me a long, rolling wake to paddle. In the distance rose the skyline of Seattle, for all its pedestrian architecture remarkably beautiful and dear.

I passed beneath Magnolia Bluff and what remained of the U.S. Navy Receiving Station at Pier 91. My father had been stationed here, and we had lived in the "quarters" high on the bluff when I was a child. When I was old enough to explore, my

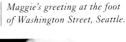

Maggie's greeting at the foot of Washington Street, Seattle.

friends and I used to pass through a gap in our chain-link fence and, feet sliding, hands reaching, scuttle down this bluff through the Scotch broom and madrona to the cobble beach below. Today the beach is a marina. The city I grew up in is a metropolis on barnacled rocks.

At the ferry piers I held up as the *Walla Walla* began her full-to-capacity run to Bainbridge; then I scooted in behind her and turned between piers toward the Pioneer Square public dock. There were a number of people on the floats, the sun bringing down the men from the missions and alleys of the original "skid road." Then there flashed a bit of color between passed-out drifters and jigging fishermen—Maggie in a pale blue skirt and patterned blouse, bright yellow flowers in one hand. I allowed Boato to drift the final yards of the journey as Maggie leaned forward with a simple "Welcome home."

Glass towers blazing, the city of Seattle confronts a kayaker.

A CONTACT GUIDE TO THE
MARINE TRAILS OF NORTH AMERICA

The idea of a water trail has spread rapidly throughout the small boat community of North America. From Maine to Vancouver, more than a hundred trails are being considered, designated, built, or paddled. Each of them is unique, not only for its waters and paths, but also for the way it came into being and the way it continues to grow. But all these trails share one common denominator—the volunteer. Without the physical and financial support of the users—clearing out tent sites, stuffing envelopes, paying dues—each of these trails would fade away. If you believe in the freedom of a small boat and the concept of a water trail, you need to get involved.

What follows is information on the water trails in North America that are already navigable. If the contacts given have changed, check with North American Water Trails Incorporated. This is an umbrella organization that also will provide the best information about existing trails in your region as well as new trails.

NORTH AMERICAN WATER TRAILS INCORPORATED

Contact: Dave Getchell, Sr., director, North American Water Trails, Inc., 56 Pease Town Road, Appleton, Maine 04862-6455; (207) 785-4079

ALLAGASH WILDERNESS WATERWAY

Location: Northwestern Maine
Description & Status: 92-mile river and lake wilderness trail with Wild and Scenic Rivers designation
Sites: 80
Fees: Nightly fee at site
Contact: The Bureau of Parks and Lands, Parks Northern Region, 106 Hogan Road, Bangor, Maine 04401; (207) 941-4014

THE MAINE ISLAND TRAIL

Location: The Maine coast between Portland and Machias Bay
Description & Status: A volunteer-developed and -maintained 335-mile trail system through rural and wilderness coastal islands. All types of watercraft.
Sites: 79 total on both private and public lands. Permission required on some sites.
Fees: Annual membership required to use the trail and sites; members receive a superb guidebook.
Contact: The Maine Island Trail Association (MITA), PO Box C, Rockland, Maine 04101-3416; (207) 596-6456

UPPER CONNECTICUT RIVER VALLEY TRAIL

Location: Bath, New Hampshire, to Vernon, Vermont
Description & Status: 150 miles, including riverine and flatwater; rural
Sites: 17
Fees: Pay on site
Contact: Bill Bridge, Upper Valley Land Trust, 19 Buck Road, Hanover, New Hampshire 03755; (603) 643-6626

THE HUDSON RIVER WATERWAY

Location: New York City to Waterford, New York
Description & Status: 140 miles long; human-powered craft only. Trail connects the tidal Hudson River to the Erie and Champlain canal systems, as well as the New York State Canal Recreationway.
Sites: 7
Fees: None except at one private campsite
Contact: Dale Campbell, Hudson River Waterway Association, 79th Street Boat Basin, Box 46, New York, New York 10024; (212) 717-6510

POTOMAC WATER TRAIL

Location: Upper Potomac River, Washington, D.C., between Georgetown and Quantico
Description & Status: 20 miles of tidewater; urban to rural
Sites: 17 sites day use, 3 overnight reserved
Fees: Membership requested: Potomac Water Trail Association
Contact: Franz Gimmler, Potomac Water Trail Association, 3410 N. Edison Street, Alexandria, Virginia 22207; (703) 241-5464

THE FLORIDA GREENWAYS AND TRAILS SYSTEM

Location: Statewide
Description & Status: More than 38 designated state canoe trails on open waterways, some using state park camping, others open camping.
Sites: Various, depending on state
Fees: Only at certain launching areas and state parks
Contact: Office of Greenways and Trails, 325 John Knox Road, Building 500, Tallahassee, Florida 32303-4124; (850) 488-3701; http://www.dep.state.fl.us/gwt

LAKE SUPERIOR WATER TRAIL

Location: The coasts of Michigan, Wisconsin, Minnesota, and Ontario

Description & Status: The most ambitious trail, involving more than 26 government agencies and a host of associations and clubs. Includes a number of established and mapped trails in both rural and wilderness settings.

Sites: Various, depending on state

Contacts: Todd Kessler, PO Box 1211, Bayfield, Wisconsin 54814; (715) 373-2817

Steve Mueller, Minnesota Water Trails, Minnesota DNR - Trails and Waterways, 500 Lafayette Road, St. Paul, Minnesota 55155; (612) 297-4955

Dean Sandell, Michigan Sect, Lake Superior Water Trail, State Forest Operations Section, PO Box 30028, Lansing, Michigan 48909; (517) 335-3338

Natalie Farmer, Canoe Ontario, 31 Corning Road, Willowdale, Ontario M2J 2L6; (416) 393-1910

INDIANA WATER TRAILS

Location: Statewide

Description & Status: 28 mapped and defined trails

Sites: Various trails have state park canoe-camping facilities

Fees: None

Contact: Streams and Trails Section, Division of Outdoor Recreation, Indiana Department of Natural Resources, 402 West Washington, Room W271, Indianapolis, Indiana 46204; (317) 232-4070; http://www.ai.org/dnr/outdoor/canoetra/index.htm.

THE BRITISH COLUMBIA MARINE TRAIL

Location: British Columbia's coast between Vancouver Island and the British Columbia mainland

Description & Status: The longterm goal is a border-to-border trail of roughly 800 miles, from southern British Columbia north to Prince Rupert (what Americans call the Inside Passage). Though the B.C. Marine Trail Association is still in the planning stages, they are building around the Provincial Parks and seeking the use of crown lands.

Sites: To be established. The Gulf Islands have the richest concentration of Provincial Parks for paddling.

Fees: Annual membership with the British Columbia Marine Trail Association: $25 for Provincial Parks, daily or by reservation

Contact: John Nelson, British Columbia Marine Trail, Suite 3851, Wolleston, Victoria, Canada V9A 5A9; (250) 920-7424; or British Columbia Marine Trail Association, Provincial Parks, South Vancouver District, B.C. Parks; (250) 391-2300

THE CASCADIA MARINE TRAIL

Location: Puget Sound and San Juan Islands, Washington

Description & Status: Trail system of more than 300 miles, extending from Olympia (southern Puget Sound) to Point Roberts (near the Canadian border), including the San Juan Islands. Intended for small, beachable human- or wind-powered watercraft.

Sites: 43

Fees: The Washington Water Trails Association is the primary builder and maintainer of the trail. A WWTA annual membership provides access to all private, county, and community-owned sites: $25 for individuals, $35 for families. State sites accessible only through a trail pass: $40 per person or $7 per paddler per night per site.

Contacts: Washington Water Trails Association, The Good Shepherd Center, 4649 Sunnyside Avenue North, Room 305, Seattle, Washington 98103-6900; (206) 545-9161; http://www.eskimo.com/~wwta

NATIVE TRAILS

Location: The world

Description & Status: A nonprofit group dedicated to exploring and mapping historic trails. Current on-water projects include:
The 700-mile Northern Forest Canoe Trail, rural to wilderness
The Mayan Canoe Routes on the Yucatan Peninsula, Mexico, rural to wilderness
The water routes of the Russian Urals to the Pacific

Fees: $25 annual fee for information on all trails; $5 for specific trails

Contact: Mike Krepner, Native Trails Inc., Box 240, Waldoboro, Maine 04572; (207) 832-5255

BIBLIOGRAPHY

Angell, Tony, and Kenneth C. Balcomb III. *Marine Birds and Mammals of Puget Sound*. Seattle: Washington Sea Grant Program, 1984:2.

Barkan, Frances B., ed. *The Wilkes Expedition: Puget Sound and the Oregon Country*. Olympia: Washington State Capital Museum, 1987.

Birkeland, Torger. *Echoes of Puget Sound: Fifty Years of Logging and Steamboating*. Caldwell, Idaho: Caxton Printers, 1960.

Blanchan, Neltje. *Bird Neighbors*. Garden City Publishing Co., 1922:102–104.

Blankenship, Georgiana. *Early History of Thurston County, Washington together with Biographies and Reminiscences of those identified with Pioneer Days*. Olympia: Shorey Book Store, 1914.

Burns, Robert. *The Shape & Form of Puget Sound*. Seattle: Washington Sea Grant Program, 1985:23–45.

Chasan, Daniel Jack. *The Water Link: A History of Puget Sound as a Resource*. Seattle: Washington Sea Grant Program, 1981.

Dyson, George B. "The Pacific Paddle Trail: A Proposal for the 1990s and Beyond." *Sea Kayaker*, winter 1987:12–13.

Getchell, David R. Sr. *Modern Water Trails: A Guide to Establishing and Maintaining Recreational Waterways*. Conference publication, North American Water Trails Conference, Appleton, Maine, 1995.

Gorsline, Jerry, ed. *Rainshadow: Archibald Menzies and the Botanical Exploration of the Olympic Peninsula*. Port Townsend, Wash.: Jefferson County Historical Society, 1992.

Hamas, Michael J. *The Belted Kingfisher*. Birds of North America Series, no. 84. Philadelphia: Academy of Natural Sciences, 1994.

Indian Claim Commission. *Tribal Distribution in Washington: Coast Salish and Western Washington Indians*. Vol. 5. New York: Garland Publishing, 1974.

Kruckeberg, Arthur R. *The Natural History of Puget Sound Country*. Seattle: University of Washington Press, 1995.

Lilly, Kenneth E. Jr. *Marine Weather of Western Washington*. Seattle: Starpath School of Navigation, 1983.

Lincoln, Leslie. *Coast Salish Canoes*. Seattle: Center for Wooden Boats, 1991.

Lynn, Howard W. *Lieutenant Maury's Island and the Quartermaster's Harbor*. Vashon Island: Beachcomber Press, 1975.

Menzies, Archibald. *Menzies' Journal of Vancouver's Voyage, April to October, 1792*, ed. C. F. Newcombe. Archives of British Columbia, Memoir no. 5. Victoria, B.C.: W. H. Cullin, 1923.

Neal, J., C. Hart, D. Lynch, S. Chan, and J. Harris. *Oil Spills in Washington State: A Historical Analysis*. Olympia: Department of Ecology Spill Management Program, 1997.

Newell, Gordon R. *Ships of the Inland Sea*. Portland, Ore.: Binfords & Mort, 1951.

Reinartz, Kay F., ed. *Passport to Ballard: The Centennial Story*. Seattle: Ballard News Tribune, 1988.

Sagerson, Mary, and Duane Robinson. *Grapeview: The Detroit of the West*. Shelton, Wash.: Mason County Historical Society, 1992.

Simpson, Peter, ed. *City of Dreams: A Guide to Port Townsend*. Port Townsend, Wash.: Bay Press, 1986.

Snyder, Warren A. *Southern Puget Sound Salish: Texts, Place Names, and Dictionary*. Sacramento: Sacramento Anthropological Society, Sacramento State College, 1968.

Steele, E. N. *The Rise and Decline of the Olympia Oyster*. Elma, Wash.: Fulco Publications, 1957.

Strickland, Richard M. *The Fertile Fjord: Plankton in Puget Sound*. Seattle: Washington Sea Grant Program, 1983.

Suttles, Wayne P. *Coast Salish Essays*. Seattle: University of Washington Press, 1987.

Van Olinda, O. S. *History of Vashon-Maury Islands*. Vashon, Wash.: Vashon Island News-Record, 1935.

Vancouver, George. *A voyage of discovery to the North Pacific Ocean and round the world, 1791–1795*. Vol. 2, ed. W. Kaye Lamb. London: Hakluyt Society, 1984.

Viola, Herman J., and Carolyn Margolis, eds. *Magnificent Voyagers: The U.S. Exploring Expedition, 1838–1842*. Washington, D.C.: Smithsonian Institution Press, 1985.

Waterman, Thomas Talbot. *Puget Sound Geography*. Special Collections, University of Washington, Seattle. Washington, D.C.: Smithsonian Office of Anthropology, 1920.

West, James E. *Protection and Restoration of Marine Life in the Inland Waters of Washington State*. Puget Sound/Georgia Strait Basin Environmental Report Series, no. 6. Olympia: Washington Work Group on Protecting Marine Life, 1997.

Wing, Robert C., and Gordon Newell. *Peter Puget*. Seattle: Gray Beard Publishing, 1979.

Wright, E. W., ed. *Lewis & Dryden's Marine History of the Pacific Northwest*. New York: Antiquarian Press, 1961.

Yates, Steve. *Orcas, Eagles & Kings: Georgia Strait and Puget Sound*. Boca Raton, Fla. and Seattle, Wash.: Primavera Press, 1992.

"The Vancouver Expedition: Peter Puget's Journal of the Exploration of Puget Sound May 7– June 11, 1792." Seattle: *Pacific Northwest Quarterly*, April 1939.

ABOUT THE AUTHOR

Sailor, timber cruiser, halibut fisherman, photojournalist—Joel W. Rogers is the consummate Northwesterner. He was raised on salmon in Seattle's Ballard neighborhood, has overhauled fishing boats on Bainbridge Island, worked as a deckhand on Puget Sound tugboats, and lived in the Skagit River estuary. In addition, Rogers has kayaked almost everywhere in Puget Sound. Author-photographer of the acclaimed *The Hidden Coast: Kayak Explorations from Alaska to Mexico*, Rogers photographs and writes about sea kayaking, rowing, and environmental issues that affect the Northwest. He lives in Seattle's Pike Place Market and stores his kayaks in Madison Park, on Lake Washington.